BEHOLD WOMAN

BEHOLD WOMAN
A Jungian Approach to Feminist Theology

for Scribner,

with much love,

Carrin.

CARRIN DUNNE

CHIRON PUBLICATIONS
Wilmette, Illinois

The Chiron Monograph Series, Volume II
General Editors: Nathan Schwartz-Salant, Murray Stein
Managing Editors: Harriet Hudnut Halliday, Siobhan Drummond Granner

Library of Congress Catalog Card Number: 88–4699

Printed in the United States of America
Edited by Harriet Hudnut Halliday
Book design by Elaine Hill

Library of Congress Cataloging-in-Publication Data:
Dunne, Carrin.
     Behold woman : a Jungian approach to feminist theology
  / Carrin Dunne.
          p. cm.
     Bibliography: p.
     Includes index.
     1. Women and religion. 2. Woman (Christian theology) I.
Title.
     BL458.D86 1988
     291'.088042--dc19   88-4699
                                                    CIP

ISBN 0–933029–37–3 (cloth)

ISBN 0–933029–38–1 (paper)

*for **James Aylward***
Socratic midwife and friend

Contents

Introduction

In October 1984 I had a strange dream. I had been pondering a psychotheological matter which I felt was really too difficult for my abilities. I had been asked to respond to Jung's critique of the Christian notions of good and evil at a conference to be sponsored by the C. G. Jung Institute of Chicago the following year. The proposed task set up a tension inside me which either provoked or called out for the dream. At least I had the immediate conviction on waking that the following dream, enigmatic as it is, would help me through my quandary.

> A woman with long dark hair and in a bright red dress has a huge, gaping hole in the upper half of her torso. It is as though it has been blasted away by a cannon shot so that her entire chest cavity is missing. She moves into the embrace of her lover and the wound is instantly healed. She asks: "Is this it?" and a voice answers: "No, that is not it." The scene repeats itself twice more. Each time she asks: "Is this it?" and the voice answers: "No, that is not it."

> In a darkened movie theater a small boy dressed in knickers, knee socks, and a touring cap is scrambling around beneath the seats, looking for a bit of film. The curl of film which he has not yet found is about twelve to fifteen inches long.

The first title I gave to the dream was *"Privatio Boni"* because at the time I was thinking about that classic expression of the Christian notion of evil as a lack or absence of good. I saw the hole in the woman's chest, the darkened theater and the lost bit of film as images of that lack, the healing embrace and the boy searching for the film as images of the good.[1] I was also aware that the dream was saying something about the situation of woman (are not the questions of woman and evil inevitably intermingled in our thoughts?) and gave it two alternative titles: "Behold Woman" and "Does Woman have a Soul?" One year later, when I presented my talk in Chicago, I was surprised at the spontaneous reaction of the women in the audience in particular to my dream images. I realized then that the dream deserved more work in the direction of what it might reveal about woman.

At first what arrested me most about the dream was the startling opening image of a live woman with a massive wound to the chest, the incongruity and the pathos of it. How could she be alive with what was so clearly a mortal wound? Who was this being who presented herself in such a dolorous way? The image of the woman called to mind that of Christ scourged, crowned with thorns, dressed in mock purple, with a reed in hand for scepter, whom Pilate presented before the people with the words: "Behold the Man" (Jn. 19:5). In Pilate's mouth the words meant: "Surely you are not threatened by the pretensions of such a one." In John's Gospel the words assume ontological and theological resonance: "Behold what it is to be human; Behold the One who sums up the very essence of humanity." The woman of my dream partakes of all these meanings. She is a pathetic figure so that the question can and indeed has been raised: "Does she have a soul?" At the same time her suffering aspect is a revelation of the ontological/theological status of the human soul. The very absence which seems to argue against besouledness is a revelation of soul. What is not, is.

My starting point is my own dream. Beginning there in my own earth, in what I take to be a personal revelation, that is, a revelation given to me and a revelation which is me, has given me the confidence and staying power to complete my task and to overcome the internal voices which murmur incessantly along the way: "You cannot do this"; "What is the point of it?"; "How dare you say such things?" Because it is my dream it gives me a right and even a call to speak. It also shows me the way. The very unfolding of the dream, following its strange sort of logic, is a guide for thought, somewhat like Ariadne's ball of thread rolling slowly through the corridors of the labyrinth. Insofar as the labyrinth describes the inner form of Mother Earth, dream logic may be a privileged mode of access to her secrets.

I must confess that I enjoy the kind of bafflement which dream images and events present to the mind. What brings my mind to a full stop also serves to stimulate it in unexpected directions. Not so enjoyable but just as necessary is the havoc it plays with my sense of propriety.

The dream makes free with both the 'is' and the 'ought,' but in so doing it affords a possibility (much as do the unforeseen and uncontrollable events of the outer world, if less implacably) of widening and deepening the scope of mind and heart. There is something also to working through one's own material which makes a difference not only psychologically, leading to greater self-awareness, but ontologically, leading to greater self-possession. Not only ontologically but theologically, for the light of revelation comes not only from without and from the past (Sacred Scripture and the collective wisdom of mankind) but from within and from the present. I find myself weaving back and forth by way of association and suggestion between my dream and the inexhaustible fund of stories which is our common inheritance, between the individual and the collective, according to a dialectic which has no rules. It is a matter of following the Spirit and of becoming spirit, insofar as spirit is relationship.[2]

It is primarily because I begin with my own dream and amplify it through what I am able to connect to the common memory of mankind that I call what I am doing "a Jungian approach." I know that feminists are somewhat leery of the Jungian propensity for archetypes which can too easily degenerate into stereotypes. The criticism is well worth heeding for the danger is ever-present, as Jung himself says.[3]

What are the differences between an archetype and a stereotype? An archetype is the original exemplar. It would be, for instance, the original woman or woman as she is in the mind of God. Not something we know from the outset, even though the word 'original' is used, but something toward which we grope, something which we struggle to approximate. The archetype works in us from the beginning, preshaping and motivating our feeling, imagining and thinking about her. It also moves us along, forcing us to question our feelings, shift our images, and correct our thoughts about her. She is the living source of any number of expressions and is as such inexpressible. We can recognize her but we cannot cognize her. In that sense my title goes too far when it says, "Behold Woman." On the other hand, my dream image of woman is not my conscious invention but came to me from unknown sources. An archetype is numinous; it attracts energy, fascinates, has presence. We imagine it as cloudlike and glowing, a shifting form whose contours dissolve in light. A stereotype is stiff, hard, resistant to change. The energy has drained out of it; it has no drawing power. We are left with a feeling of flatness, a lack of vitality—"Is this all there is?" Our attention wanders. If nothing else, we know the difference between an archetype and a stereotype by the effect each has upon us. When the image emerges from the unconscious, that is, from we know not where, there is at least a chance of freshness, particularly if we allow ourselves to be led by the image as it moves of its own accord instead of forcing it along well-worn paths.

The business of amplification (finding connections between a dream image and associated images, between a dream story and associated stories) is not without its problems too. I sometimes feel that Jung's own writings tend to bog down in a veritable thicket of amplifications. I lose sight of the forest for all the trees. In the last analysis, everything connects to everything else and the mind goes numb trying to follow all the connections. But how to choose without oversimplifying and distorting the picture, thus stereotyping? I don't see any way to avoid a certain arbitrariness of choice while remaining humanly intelligible. My vision of woman is necessarily a limited vision, reflecting the woman I am. My hope is that my light, however small, may spark other lights, other visions, so that more and more of the entire circuitry may appear in all its vast array of colors. The mode of choice is free form. I allow my mind and heart to play, to move where they will. I don't know where these movements come from nor where they are going, but I watch them with close attention and map them as best I can. A discovery process, a mode of becoming, a way of carrying forward while being woven back into the divine comedy which is the story of humankind.

Working this way through dream and story, I have found it difficult, often impossible to make clear lines of demarcation between woman as idea and a real woman, between woman's soul and woman as soul, between the heavenly woman (the feminine aspect of God) and the earthly woman (her fallenness). The same image of the woman with the hole in her chest can be viewed in all these ways, and I find myself moving back and forth between the one and the other. This too may be an effect of working with an archetype. Mirrors which are also windows, we move through the looking-glass back and forth between worlds. Soulish reality, midway between heaven and earth, looks both ways. What I am attempting to do is both psychology and theology, but in an undogmatic, personal, exploratory sort of way. A way of rubbing both sides of the coin: "that I may know myself, that I may know Thee; that I may return into myself and into Thee."[4]

Endnotes

1. For a preliminary adumbration of the dream in relation to the problem of good and evil see my "Between Two Thieves: A Response to Jung's Critique of the Christian Notions of Good and Evil" in *Jung's Challenge to Contemporary Religion*, Murray Stein and Robert L. Moore, eds., (Wilmette, Ill.: Chiron Publications, 1987), pp. 19–21.
2. Cf. Kierkegaard on spirit as relationship in *Sickness unto Death*, Part I, section A.
3. "The ground principles, the *archai*, of the unconscious are indescribable because of their wealth of reference, although in themselves recognisable. The discriminating intellect naturally keeps on trying to establish their singleness of meaning and thus misses the essential point; for what we can above all establish as the one thing consistent with their nature is their *manifold meaning* [Jung's underlining], their almost limitless wealth of reference, which makes any unilateral formulation impossible." C. G. Jung, 1934. Archetypes of the Collective Unconscious. In *Collected Works*, 9 i:80. (Princeton: Princeton University Press, 1968). References to the *Collected Works* are by volume and paragraph.
4. St. Augustine, *Soliloquies*, II, 1 and 6.

Chapter One

Does Woman Have a Soul?
(Five Approaches to an Image)

Each time I come upon this question in the writings of C. G. Jung my anger flares. How could such a question even be raised? How could it have been, according to Jung, debated seriously in medieval seminaries? Jung calls it a famous question; I call it a famous/infamous question. The dream image of the woman with a hole in her chest makes it "my question."

On the one hand, the question is outrageous. On the other hand, my dream indicates to me that there must be a certain appropriateness or truth to the question, whether that truth be a historical accident, something which has befallen woman over the course of time, or an inherent truth arising from the very nature of woman. The woman's entire chest cavity is missing, which means that most of her vital organs are gone, a strange but fitting image for a missing soul or life-principle. The dream analogy ("it is as though it has been blasted away by a cannon shot") points in the direction of historical accident, as does the feeling of outrage, though the fact that it could happen, that her having a soul could be placed in question or that it could be blasted away, may have something to do with the very nature of woman.

The verb 'blast' comes from a root meaning 'to blow'. In its primary meaning it is a violent gust of wind. It suggests that there may be some opposition between wind or spirit (the *ruach Yahweh*) and soul. Was her soul blown away with the advent of spirit? A cannon is a weapon of warfare, heavy artillery, phallic both in form and in action, or as 'canon' it has to do with church law and with the circle of priests around the bishop who together form a cathedral chapter. All that is 'canonical' (the rod, the rule, the authorized books of the Bible, the canonization process which sets the standards of sanctity) is somehow inimical to her. The cannon fires and blasts a hole in her chest. The

1

super-male turns her into a super-female by exaggerating the feminine principle, the hole, now extended from the genital region to the upper register, specifically to the domain of the heart-lung *chakra*. It brings to mind in a curious way the figure of Sheela-na-gig, which adorns medieval churches in Ireland and England. The Sheela holds open a greatly outsized vagina; she is, as it were, almost all hole.

The heart chakra (Eros) is her proper domain, just as the throat chakra (Logos) is proper to the male. Together these middle chakras form the specific region of soul as mediator between body (the three lower chakras or drives) and spirit (the two upper chakras or gifts). It is noteworthy that she is wounded in what is proper to her. It is also noteworthy that the wounding serves to enlarge her in her own being (as "hole"). It may even turn out to be a blessing, a hint carried along in the stream of language where in French to wound is *blesser,* a wound is a *blessure.*

1

The image of a wound, and particularly of a wound to the soul, brings to mind the Catholic doctrine of original sin as a "wounding" of human nature. It takes us back to the Garden of Eden and to the drama of the Fall with its four principal players: God, the man, the woman, and the serpent. As we know from the account in Genesis, God spoke primarily to the man while the serpent addressed the woman. There are other Biblical passages, both in the Old and New Testaments (specifically Nm. 21:4−9 and Jn. 3:14), which hint broadly that God and the serpent are not altogether separate. In fact, if we were to think in Greek terms, we might say that the serpent is God's animal form, as is the owl for Athena or the cow for Hera. Nevertheless, God and the serpent are at apparent cross-purposes in the drama of the Garden, which is to say that a conflict is occurring in God in which the man and the woman will be both battlefield and victim, and perhaps eventually redeemer and redemptrix.

Where does the wounding occur? What shape does it take? From the male perspective they are first affected in terms of their awareness, the Logos factor ("the eyes of them both were opened, and they knew that they were naked"), and consequently in terms of their relationships, the Eros factor ("and they sewed fig leaves together, and made themselves aprons. And they heard the voice of the Lord God walking in the garden in the cool of the day: and Adam and his wife

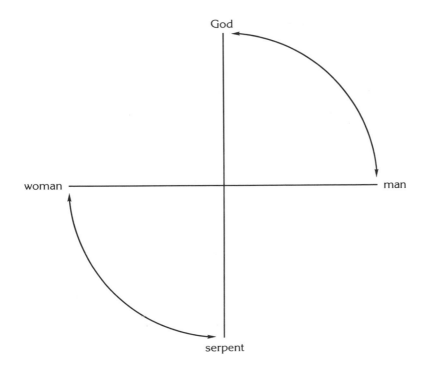

hid themselves from the presence of the Lord God amongst the trees of the garden" [Gn. 3:7–8]). An awareness of nakedness is a complex awareness, including both sexual awakening with all the complications it presents and an awareness of vulnerability (woundability), the threat of exposure, of helplessness, even of absurdity.[1] The reaction is to hide (with all the complications it presents) from one another and from God. The simplicity and harmony of Paradise were lost in that instant of complex awareness and withdrawal; self-consciousness and all the arts of civilization were gained. Did the serpent lie? Or were their eyes indeed opened, so that they became "as gods, knowing good and evil" (3:5)? Did God's threat ("in the day that thou eatest thereof thou shalt surely die" [2:17]) come to pass? They did not die on the spot, but worse, they became aware of death and of the connection between life and death, and they recoiled.

But what is the female perspective on the Fall? The awareness and recoil which constitute the masculine dimension of the Fall from grace correspond to a "blessing" promised by God when He addresses the serpent. "I will put enmity between thee and the woman, and between thy seed and her seed; it shall bruise thy head, and thou shalt bruise its [or his] heel" (3:15). From her point of view they are affected primarily in the domain of Eros, and the most hurtful break of relationship occurs between herself and the serpent, then between herself and the man, and finally between both of them and God. From time out of mind she had been intimate to the point of identification with the serpent; now that relationship is ruptured when Nature itself in the guise of the serpent conspires to cast them out through their newly found self-consciousness. "The serpent beguiled me ..." (3:13). The other side of the complex consciousness gained through an awareness of nakedness is a loss of natural mind, woman's mind, the wisdom of the serpent ("Now the serpent was more subtil[2] than any beast of the field which the Lord God had made" [3:1]), symbolized by the bruising of the serpent's head. The lack of natural wisdom is man's Achilles' heel.

It is only recently with the advent of modern psychology that we have begun to think (very cautiously) that part of the fault for the Fall belongs to God, that Paradise was a "set up." The serpent, however, has been blamed at least from the time of the writing of the Genesis story, and probably long before that, if we think of how Gilgamesh rejected the Goddess and eventually lost the herb of immortality to a serpent. By New Testament times the serpent had become identified with the devil, the archetypal enemy (Satan), a tempter, a liar, a murderer. Now if the serpent is woman's own mind, the symbol of her soul, how difficult will it be for her, particularly if she is civilized and/or religious, to find her own mind and to embrace her own self? It would be like deliberately embracing sin, all that is anti-God; it would be choosing witchery. No wonder that as civilization progresses it becomes increasingly questionable whether or not she has a soul.

God asks the man, "Who told thee that thou wast naked?" (3:11). The man points to the woman; the woman points to the serpent; the successive gesture reveals to God His own nakedness. Can God handle the revelation? God sows distrust between the man and his wife, and concomitantly between the man and his own soul—"Because thou hast hearkened unto the voice of thy wife ..." (3:17). Why doesn't God say in like manner to the woman, "Because thou hast hearkened unto the voice of the serpent ..."? Is it because it would be too much like saying "Because thou hast listened to me, because thou hast heard me too well, because thou hast overheard that part of me which I do not care to acknowledge ..."? Instead God curses the serpent, reducing it from *arum* (wisdom) to *arur* (misery). "Because thou hast done this,

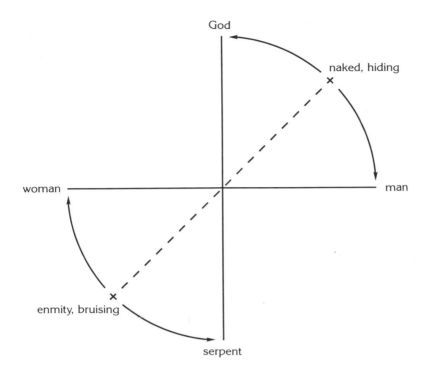

thou art cursed above all cattle, and above every beast of the field; upon thy belly shalt thou go, and dust shalt thou eat all the days of thy life" (3:14). There is a reminder here of the close connection between the sexual organs and the organs of excretion ("dust shalt thou eat"), and therefore between sexuality and death ("for dust thou art, and unto dust shalt thou return" [3:19]).

In what does the sin of the woman consist? Is it that she disobeyed the ban of God? Is it that she hearkened to the voice of the serpent? God does not condemn her in these terms. He asks: "What is this that thou hast done?" She answers: "The serpent beguiled me, and I did eat" (3:13). Does her sin consist in eating the forbidden fruit, in eating it in bad conscience, or in betraying the serpent? If we look upon her as a human being, the answer would most probably be "all of the above"; if we look upon her more specifically as a woman, our first answer will be that she betrayed the serpent. Either way she suffers a profound dislocation from her deepest self. She is torn between God-as-serpent and God-as-God, and is faithful neither to the one nor to the other.

"The serpent beguiled me. . . ." All the words we use to express the wisdom of the serpent have a predominantly pejorative cast. The serpent mind is guileful, wily, treacherous, tricky, subtle, insidious, cunning, crafty, clever, sly, shrewd, astute, artful, ingenious. It suggests a superior intelligence, but one that is amoral if not immoral, a mind not ordained to the good. Small wonder that in the ancient story of Inanna and the *Huluppu*-Tree,[3] Inanna, who finds the primordial Tree, which is herself, and plants it in her garden, which is herself, weeps over the self that she discovers, for a serpent who could not be charmed made its nest in the roots, the *Anzu*-bird set its young in the branches, and Lilith inhabited the trunk. She calls upon her hero, Gilgamesh, to chop down the tree with his bronze axe. Civilized woman is as horrified at the sight of herself as is civilized man at the sight of her. But in her anxiety to disown the frightful vision, which according to Greek myth turns man to stone, she loses sight of herself. Out of sight, out of mind. The sum total of her effort is a loss of mind, not in the sense of insanity, though that happens too, but in a loss of the intelligence proper to her. There can be no doubt that, whatever the question *"Habet mulier animam?"* implies for Jung, for the medieval theologians who raised it woman was thought to be of inferior and weak intelligence.[4]

Perhaps it would be more correct to say that where fallen woman "feels" her loss most acutely is in the realm of mind. That blank and empty place aggravates in her a desire for the world of men where mind sparkles so brilliantly and easily: "and thy desire shall be to thy husband, and he shall rule over thee" (3:16). He rules over her because when she tries to think as he thinks, her thoughts are derivative, second-rate. It is not that she is intellectually his inferior. What is askew in her has to do with relationship first of all, the domain in which she appears to have retained some expertise. But where a disease manifests is not always its primary site, and until the disease is treated at its root the symptoms will merely shift. Her wound is not in the throat area, as might be supposed from her historical inability to express herself. She has lost heart and lungs (and breasts), liver, stomach and spleen. She has turned away from her origin and original mind, God-as-serpent. Until that most fundamental relationship is healed, she is lost to herself and therefore lost (really if not apparently) to others.

Can the serpent be redeemed? If the serpentine mind is amoral, would it not be immoral, even an outright rejection of morality, for her to turn back to her primitive consciousness? An answer, or at least an orientation, may be found in a neglected saying of Jesus: "Behold, I send you forth as sheep in the midst of wolves: be ye therefore wise as serpents, and harmless as doves" (Mt. 10:16). What is dangerous about the serpent mind is not the superior intelligence nor the artfulness, but the intention to do harm. Consider the more concrete meanings of some of the adjectives used to describe the serpent wisdom: 'insidious' means to lie in wait; 'sly' means able to strike; 'cunning' means able, full of know-how, but also conning; 'guile' or 'wile' refers to divination, sorcery, and the casting of spells (through the Old English *wigle* there may even be a distant reference to the wiggle or sinuous motion of the snake); 'subtle' means thin or fine, able to slip in or slip by unnoticed; 'crafty' means strong; 'ingenious' refers to inborn talent or skill; 'shrewd' has to do with the intelligence of the nose (intuition). These qualities can serve not only to frighten but to delight. When we think of what makes one piece more artful than another, is it not the ability to take us by surprise, a sudden showing forth of the unexpected, and an ability to hold us, as it were, under a spell? The question is whether we can afford to surrender ourselves to the delight without its proving our undoing. What makes the difference is whether or not the wisdom of the serpent is combined with the harmlessness of the dove.

Harmlessness requires the abandonment of intention, even so-called good intentions. Given the potentially infinite scope of human being, any attempt to use another human being for one's own purposes, whatever they may be, is limiting and therefore harmful. The antidote is formulated most succinctly by the *I Ching* when speaking of the female divine principle where it functions at its best: "Without purpose,/ Yet nothing remains unfurthered" (hexagram 2, line 2). To be without purpose is a large order, a feat which may indeed be more divine than human. It is not achieved merely by ignoring one's purposes, averting one's attention from the unconscious motives. In that regard the King James rendering of "harmless" shows its superiority to "innocent," which just means not knowing. To make the unconscious conscious, to move from innocence (in the negative sense) to awareness—one of the major goals of Freudian and Jungian psychologies—is the truly human step on the way from innocence to harmlessness. The second step, the actual abandonment of selfish purpose once unmasked, remains a divine secret or a divine gift, but that the wisdom of the serpent can be coupled with the harmlessness of the dove is hinted at by language itself which mixes 'ingenious' (referring to an inventive, cunning, and brilliant mind) with 'ingenuous' (referring to an open, honest, candid, unsophisticated mind) to get 'ingenuity'. True genius lies in that miraculous combination.

2

In the days of the Goddess when Gilgamesh and his friend, Enkidu, chopped down her cedar forest and destroyed its guardian, Humbaba, her desire was awakened for Gilgamesh.[5] Why was she not rather infuriated at the desecration of the Tree which is herself? Why did she in fact call upon Gilgamesh to cut down her *Huluppu*-Tree? The fury will come later, much later. At the moment she is grateful to her liberator for she has already (in the beginning, prior to the story) turned away from herself. It is the "original" sin or sundering which she herself commits against herself, even if another hand holds the axe which wounds her. The story of the *Huluppu*-Tree gives a clearer idea of why she turned in horror from herself. Its tangled roots are the snake which cannot be charmed, its strong body Lilith, its reaching branches the *Anzu*-bird and its young.

What is the *Anzu*-bird? Whatever it may have been for the ancient Sumerians,[6] its correspondent in Egypt is the vulture. We think of the vulture as an ugly bird with a naked head, made uglier by its associations with death. The sight of vultures feasting on the carcass of man or beast is a grim reminder of our mortality. What woman would want to be compared with a vulture? What modern nation would choose as its emblem the vulture or the snake? yet these were the sacred emblems of Upper and Lower Egypt from earliest times. Nekhbet the vulture Goddess was protectress of Upper Egypt, while Wadjet the "green one" or snake Goddess, was protectress of Lower Egypt. The king as Lord of the "Two Lands" wore a double crown, called the *pschent,* embodying the combined powers of the snake and vulture Goddesses. In predynastic Egypt and in ancient Sumer, prior to the time of the Gilgamesh epic and to the story of Inanna and the *Huluppu*-Tree, there must have been a very different feeling toward the snake and the vulture, probably corresponding to a radically different attitude toward life and death.

It is most interesting that in historic times right on through to the present day the eagle is much admired. How is it that we admire the devourer of living flesh but turn shuddering from the devourer of the dead? Is it that we are more horrified by decomposition and decay than by killing? Only since modern psychology of religion has, through a study of the alchemical process and of shamanic initiation rediscovered the inner meaning and positive purpose of decomposition, has there been to a change of feeling in this regard. To undergo the breakdown of a life structure that has become rigid and nonfunctional may be frightening and painful, but it is also to experience a most wonderful "release of soul." The ancient Egyptians preceived the work of the vulture, which aids and hastens the process, as motherly. She who is not put off by the smelly diapers of the newborn, prepared as she is by long familiarity with the smelliness of her own menses, is not rebuffed by the odor of putrefaction. The Aztecs had a Goddess known as "Filth Eater" to whom they confessed their sins. She had deep affinities to Mary, the Virgin Mother of God, under her title "Refuge of Sinners," and both hark back to the kindly vulture Goddess. She is in some ways an even more salvific image than the sacrificed Lamb of God who takes away the sins of the world, which leaves us with an even graver sin and heavier guilt.

In early times all vultures were thought to be female, probably because the work of the vulture is so deeply associated with the feminine divine principle. They were fecundated by the wind. Thus the vulture comes to stand for the female in her own right, apart from the male, and for a spirituality which is her own. A later vulture Goddess, Mut, was thought to be married to Amun, the "hidden one," the effective force in the invisible wind. The spirit that works through her is the wind that "bloweth where it listeth, and thou hearest the sound thereof, but canst not tell whence it cometh, and whither it goeth" (Jn.3:8). She is also the brooding presence over the primeval waters (Gn.1:2), for while vultures do not fly as high as eagles, they are beautiful fliers, catching the thermal updrafts and appearing to hover endlessly and effortlessly, looking not to the sky but to the earth with maternal solicitude.

It seems strange, despite the unattractive appearance of the vulture, that Inanna would not want to claim her sublime qualities. I can only imagine that it is because of our terror of coming apart, of falling into pieces, the horror of unbecoming which must precede any new creation. And then there is the factor of uncontrollability, that of the spirit which moves her of which even she cannot tell "whence it cometh, and whither it goeth."

Lilith, or Lilake, is mentioned only this once in extant Sumerian literature and only once in the Bible (Is. 34:14–15), but we know her from Hebrew legend. As in the fairy tales, God tried three times before He was able to make a suitable mate for Adam.[7] His first try was Lilith, who was made not from Adam's rib but, like Adam, from the earth, though Adam was made from pure dust while Lilith was made from slime. What is pure about dust? And what is filthy about slime?

Dust is fine particulate matter. It has no strong smell, though it can clog the nostrils and throat when it rises in clouds. it is matter, dirt, but we are easily rid of it by brushing or wiping. It is the most ethereal form of dirt, approaching air, even light, which is made visible through dust motes. Slime, on the other hand, is slick, slippery (resembling the snake), and sticky, hard to be rid of once it is on you. It is very close to, if not actually made up of, bodily fluids: mucous, secretions, excrement, bird lime, slug trails, ooze. It is viscous matter in the early stages of decomposition giving off noisome and noxious gases.

We can get a better idea of the reality of Lilith by comparison with God's second and third attempts. After Lilith had deserted Adam, God tried again and let Adam watch as He put together a woman out of bone, blood, muscle, tissue, and organs, covering the whole with skin and tufts of hair. Adam was overcome by disgust at this inside view of the material side of his nature, so God took the second woman away, put Adam into a deep sleep, and fashioned Eve from his rib. With Eve he was delighted, not only because she was closer to being part of him, but because he had not had to look at the out-of-which she had come. If the second woman was repugnant to him, we can only imagine that Lilith is even closer to *prima materia,* which is according to the great 13th century theologian, St. Thomas Aquinas, the very antithesis of God: "one [God] is pure act, the other [prime matter] is pure potency, and they agree in nothing" (*Summa Contra Gentiles* I, 17). Thomas called David of Dinant's opinion that God is to be found in prime matter "madness," forgetting that "he hath regarded the low estate of his handmaiden" (Lk. 1:48).

Despite her associations with the primeval ooze, in the story of the *Huluppu*-Tree, Lilith, occupying as she does the middle range of the Tree, is the most human of its inhabitants. On a Sumerian terracotta relief dating from 2000 B.C. she is pictured naked, holding something like an ankh symbol in either hand, with bird feet, standing on two hyenas and flanked by owls. Isaiah gives her for companions jackals, ostriches, wild cats, hyenas, and, of course, the snake and the vulture. With the exception of the snake, which is life-and-death, they are omens of death and inhabitants of wild, desolate places. According to Jewish legend, Lilith forsook Adam when he insisted that she assume the subordinate position in their lovemaking. It is an earthier and yet more human version of Lilith's fleeing the *Huluppu*-Tree when Gilgamesh lays his bronze axe to it. She is nature untamed and untameable. When Gilgamesh carves a throne and a bed for Inanna from the wood of the *Huluppu*-Tree, Lilith is that part of the Tree which remains uncarved. She is the Taoist "uncarved block." She flees or flies (since she is winged) to the Red Sea, the transition place between Egypt and the Land of

Promise. As mistress of transitions she is uncanny and dangerous, the guardian not only of death and night (from a play on the resemblance between her name and the Hebrew *layil,* night), but of birth and life. She watches over baby boys until the eighth day, the day of circumcision when the knife is laid to their tree, and over baby girls until the twentieth day. Two is the number of femininity and ten is a perfect number, so twenty is feminine perfection. It can be seen from the difference between eight and twenty that Lilith, or Nature herself, has generally a much stronger hold on the female sex than on the male.

When the women of Jerusalem weep over Jesus, he quotes them a proverb: "if they do these things in a green tree, what shall be done in the dry?" (Lk. 23:31) It is interesting that he identifies with the green tree, where dwell the snake which cannot be charmed, the *Anzu*-bird and Lilith, rather than with the hewn tree, Inanna's throne and bed. It seems to go along with his empathy for tax-collectors and prostitutes and for what of God remains outside the Law. But Inanna prefers the hewn tree. She wants to be the throne and the bed, not the snake, the vulture, and Lilith. She wants to be civilized, admirable, and desirable to men, not uncouth, wild, sluttish, treacherous, and a reminder of all that is outside our control.

Jesus operates a turnaround on Inanna's perspective. He is the green tree nailed to the hewn tree, which is his throne and his bed. There is in the joining of the two trees—even if that joining be wrought by violence—an image for our contemplation. In the Garden of Eden there were two trees planted in the middle, the Tree of Knowledge and the Tree of Life. Oddly, no one takes notice of the Tree of Life until after the Fall. Then God says, "Behold, the man is become as one of us, to know good and evil: and now, lest he put forth his hand, and take also of the tree of life, and eat, and live for ever . . ." (Gn. 3:22). There follows the banishing. It is as though partaking of the Tree of Life does not emerge as a genuine possibility until after sin with the kind of complex awareness and disrelationship it entails. It casts some light on why the serpent apparently turns against itself in prompting the woman to seek knowledge. Nature turns against nature for the sake of civilization, but finally with a view to greater life, a recovery of nature at a higher level, where the green tree and the hewn tree are joined. In Proverbs 3:18 the Tree of Life is identified with wisdom, which occurs in a joining of opposites. There is an icon of Holy Wisdom from the Novgorod school (16th c.), which depicts Sophia winged and crowned, dressed in red like the woman of my dream, and with fiery red wings and skin. Her halo is green, while the circular mandala which contains her is green-gold. She is flanked by the Virgin and Child to her left and John the Baptist to her right, both of whom are also haloed in green. Above the head of Sophia is a bust of Christ with arms opened and extended toward her. Above Christ is an empty throne surrounded by angels. To me the figure of Sophia, here distinguished explicitly from the Virgin but identified implicitly with the throne, is strangely reminiscent of Lilith, but of a Lilith exalted and redeemed.

3

Immediately after the desecration of the cedar forest and the destruction of its guardian, the Goddess approaches Gilgamesh and offers herself in marriage. Gilgamesh replies: "Which of your lovers did you ever love forever?" Then he proceeds to recount the unhappy fate of her past lovers: Tammuz (Dumuzi) had to take her place in the netherworld, she broke the wing of the many-colored shepherd bird, dug a pit for the lion, whipped the horse, turned the shepherd into a wolf, the gardener into a blind mole. "And if you and I should be lovers, should not I be served in the same fashion as all these others whom you loved once?"[8] In his heart of hearts Gilgamesh may know, or at least suspect, that his and Enkidu's plundering of the Land of the Living, her own domain, cannot go forever unpunished, even if a part of her wants civilizing.

But to add insult to injury, was it not folly on his part? The truth of the matter is that he was caught in a double bind. Had he acceded to her wishes, he would have doubtless shared a fate similar to that of her other lovers. But by rejecting her, he kindles her wrath and must ultimately suffer the loss of his brother and friend, his animal half, his bodily life, Enkidu. As the saying goes, she hits him where it hurts the most. But what could the hapless Gilgamesh have done to avoid her treachery unscathed? First she herself calls upon him to cut down her *Huluppu*-Tree. Having done that (and what would have happened to him had he refused?),[9] Gilgamesh falls into her trap "damned if he does and damned if he doesn't."

Is the Goddess "soulless"? Is it this heartlessness he has in mind when man questions whether or not woman has a soul?

It is perhaps the common human experience to be loved and fostered by nature and then, at a certain point, when our usefulness is done, to be cast aside. We know our dependence on her, we know the joy of her, but we also know her appalling cruelty. Gilgamesh is a man with a certain maturity. He is not to be duped as her earlier lovers were. Where he falls short is in thinking he can reject her advances and in one simple move avoid her trap, either by refusing her outright, as he does at the moment of their encounter, or by giving her her due in the most peremptory and contemptuous manner, as does Enkidu after she has sent the Bull of Heaven against them, when he tosses the choice portion in her face saying, "If I could lay my hands on you, it is this I should do to you, and lash your entrails to your side."[10] By despising her, they awaken her darkest anger and a will to show them just how awful she can be.

Yet not all of her earlier lovers had been duped; some of them had gone "gentle into that good night" wittingly. There is evidence that the national shrines of Upper and Lower Egypt, the principal seats of worship of the vulture Goddess Nekhbet and the snake Goddess Wadjet, were built in the form of a hunter's trap[11] into which the initiate would enter knowingly and willingly as into the abyss of the netherworld to wend his or her way through the unknown, to find the way to the center or to emerge again to another life. We know of the Cretan labyrinth and there is a terra-cotta mask of Humbaba, the guardian of Inanna's cedar forest whom Gilgamesh and Enkidu killed, in the form of a maze, which indicates that the religion of the Goddess had developed to the level of wisdom throughout the Mediterranean world, if not throughout the world at large.

The inclusion of the Forest Journey in the epic of Gilgamesh indicates to me that Gilgamesh and Enkidu had tried the wisdom of the Goddess and found it wanting. In their story we find typified an historic turn taken by the West at the close of the age of the Bull and the beginning of the age of the Ram. It is a turn away from the Goddess to the God. Who can judge such a turn, which has brought to the West such abundant achievement and such sorrow (eerily predicted by Gilgamesh's long series of adventures and his ultimate defeat)? Has the God been any kinder than the Goddess? We who stand at the close of the age of the Fish and the beginning of the age of the Water-Bearer may feel toward the God somewhat the way Gilgamesh felt toward the Goddess.

In the fifth poem of the *Tao Te Ching,* Lao Tzu tells us that "Heaven [the God] and Earth [the Goddess] are ruthless/ They treat all things like straw dogs." The expression which Lao Tzu uses is *pu jên* (1, 2), not humane, unkind, unfeeling. It is a direct counter to Confucius' ideal of *jên,* an unselfish love which forms the foundation of human virtue. Heaven and Earth are ruthless in different ways, as evidenced by the observation that men tend to be more repulsed by the ruthlessness of the Goddess, while women tend to be more repulsed by the ruthlessness of the God. Either way, whether we are confronted by the Great Above or the Great Below, what we hold dearest is threatened and put into question. Lao Tzu continues with distressing serenity: "The sage is ruthless/ He treats people [himself included] like straw dogs." Is the solution to the awful prospect of divine soullessness to become soulless ourselves?

The word 'ruth', the first meaning of which is compassion or pity, comes for the same root (*kreu-*) as the word 'cruel'. It is an example of *t'ai chi* (3) where a thing is both itself and its opposite. 'Ruth' is half compassion and half cruelty. Compassion gives way to cruelty and cruelty gives way to compassion. In the compassion there is a hidden cruelty and in the cruelty there is a hidden compassion. There is no essential difference between 'ruth' and 'ruthless', only a difference of accent. Or it is a difference of action and passion, suggested by the two root meanings of **kreu-,* "to push or strike" emphasizing what we call the ruthless or active mode and "raw flesh" emphasizing the ruthful or passive mode. Divine compassion envelops human cruelty; human compassion nurses the wound of divine cruelty. We can identify compassion as the divine reality and cruelty as the human, or we can identify compassion as the human reality and cruelty as the divine. Or we can see both together as in the *t'ai chi,* and then we have soul. The interplay of opposites pervades our human world, and so the whole world is potentially soul. Yet, it is only when the opposites are held together consciously that an actualization of soul occurs.

In the Bible the Book of Ruth opens against a backdrop of divine cruelty. A famine in Israel forces Elimelech to migrate with his wife,

1. 不   pu—not; with *jên,* not humane, unkind, unfeeling. (Chinese)

2. 仁   jên—unselfish love, the basis of human virtue. (Chinese)

3. ☯   t'ai chi—a symbol for the process whereby a thing that is both itself and its opposite. (Chinese)

Naomi, and two sons to the land of Moab. There Elimelech dies, and ten years later the two sons, who have taken Moabite wives, also die, both childless. Left are three childless widows—Naomi and her two daughters-in-law, Ruth and Orpah. Naomi sums up the situation: "the hand of the Lord is gone out against me" (1:13). But her reaction to this series of blows is to counteract cruelty with compassion. When she arises to return to her native land, her daughters-in-law make ready dutifully to accompany her, but she absolves them of any further duty toward herself and urges them to return to their mothers and to take new husbands. She does not want them to ruin their futures for her sake. Naomi's compassion toward her daughters-in-law involves a necessary cruelty toward herself. Still, while her move is generous and humane, it bespeaks the kind of love we expect the older generation to show the younger. Then the truly unexpected occurs. While Orpah returns to her people, as is her right, Ruth insists:

Intreat me not to leave thee, or to return from following after
thee: for whither thou goest, I will go; and where thou
lodgest, I will lodge: thy people shall be my people, and thy
God my God: where thou diest, will I die, and there will I be
buried: the Lord do so to me, and more also, if ought but
death part thee and me. (1:16–17)

We do not know what motivates Ruth to such an unusual decision, for the story is silent on this point. In the thoroughly patriarchal context of the story, it makes no human sense. A woman, a foreigner, a childless widow, she will be utterly without status. What are we to make of events which fall outside the bounds of human sense, whether beyond or beneath? One possibility is that they are divine rather than human. Not external and uncontrollable "acts of God," like famine, exile, death, barrenness, but an inward impulsion which is as irresistible as it is inexplicable. It is a moment of divine enantiodromia and the turning point of the story, though it is not yet clearly so to Naomi, who, upon her return to Bethlehem, tells old friends and acquaintances: "Call me not Naomi [pleasant], call me Mara [bitter]: for the Almighty hath dealt very bitterly with me" (1:20). That a change has occurred begins to dawn on her after Ruth "happens" (2:3) to glean in the fields of Boaz, who is a kinsman of Elimelech. Meanwhile another avenue of divine compassion begins to assert itself in the form of the Torah, which gives the poor the right to glean the fields after the harvesters, and which provides for the childless dead that a kinsman shall marry the widow and bring a child into the world to carry on the dead man's name.

Naomi comes to life when she discovers with whom Ruth did her gleaning. It is in that moment that she recognizes the divine character of "the turn of events," for she cries: "Blessed be he of the Lord, who hath not left off his kindness to the living and to the dead" (2:20). It may be that another part of her joy is the sudden realization that she may be able to repay Ruth's compassion toward her. From mother-in-law she will become mother to Ruth, just as from daughter-in-law Ruth had become daughter to her. We have here in the ancient story an intimation of the feminine divine mysteries, which have been lost to the West since the closing of the sanctuary of Eleusis in the fourth century A.D. Naomi as wise woman shows Ruth how to present herself to Boaz in such a way that he will look favorably upon her, though, if truth be told, it has already been accomplished beyond the range of female machinations. When he first discovered her in his fields and learned who she was, Boaz said to her:

> It hath fully been shewed me, all that thou hast done unto thy mother-in-law since the death of thine husband: and how thou hast left thy father and thy mother, and the land of thy nativity, and art come unto a people thou knewest not heretofore. The Lord recompense thy work, and a full reward be given thee of the Lord God of Israel, under whose wings thou art come to trust." (2:11–12)

It is the divine compassion which Boaz perceives in Ruth, indistinguishable from her own highest self, which draws him to her. That same compassion reaches its climax when their marriage is blessed with a son who will be grandfather to David and ancestor to the Messiah.

Returning to Lao Tzu's fifth poem we can find there an unusual but apt image for soul, one which sheds light both on my guiding image of the woman with the hole in her chest and on the relationship between divine ruthlessness and human soul (or ruth).

> Between Heaven and Earth
> Something plays/blows like a bellows,
> Empty but unabashed;
> The more it works, the more it yields.

In these short verses there is condensed a remarkable teaching concerning soul, which is never named as such. Soul appears (or fails to "appear") as something "between" Heaven and Earth. Heaven and Earth are what make themselves felt as irresistible presences or forces. Perhaps that is why they are called divine. Great Yang and Great Yin are the really real, while what occurs between them is rather vague, formless, just a "something." The Chinese character *hsü* (1), here translated "empty," means false, untrue, unreal, hollow, empty, vacant, insubstantial, figurative, abstract. It sums up our worst fears about ourselves and our works as ephemeral, unreal, pointless. *Hsü* is used in combination with other characters to indicate falsehood, empty show, vanity, illusion, treachery, empty talk, silly fears, but it is also used to describe the quietness of meditation, humility, and purity. In Christianity it is used to express the doctrine of the Kenosis (cf. Ph. 2) and the beatitude of poverty of spirit, while in Buddhism it is the Great Void. The character is made up of the tiger (2), the old form being (3), representing tiger stripes. In geomancy it is used to indicate Yin, with an accent on the mutability of nature which changes the way a tiger changes its stripes. It is also associated with the shifting movements of the wind. The tiger surmounts inverted double dippers (4),[12] which are pouring out their contents—an emptying process, but one which will trigger growth and plenty. *Hsü* is also used to name the eleventh constellation of the Chinese calendar, corresponding to our Gemini, a repetition of the Heaven/Earth dyad and what is implicitly "between" them.

Human soul runs the entire gamut of emptiness from the absurd to the sublime and back again. It is empty but unabashed, *pu ch'u* (5, 6), not crouching or bent down, indomitable, not subjected to wrong,

1. 虛   hsü—"empty," that is, false, untrue, unreal, hollow, vacant, insubstantial, figurative, abstract. (Chinese)

2. 虎   the tiger.

3. 𧇃   old form of (2).

4. 业   inverted double dippers, pouring out, emptying.

5. 不   pu—not. (Chinese)

6. 屈   ch'u—with *pu*, not crouching or bent down, indomitable, not subjected to wrong, injustice, or grievance. (Chinese)

injustice or grievance (not bashed). Heaven and Earth exert pressure, they are opposing forces, but that force field ("raw flesh") which we call soul is constituted rather than bruised and bashed by the conflict. These forces work soul like two hands kneading dough causing it to produce, which brings us to the usual translation of *pu ch'u* as "inexhaustible," probably derived from the paradoxical combination of (1), which is a corpse or one who impersonates the dead ancestors at a sacrifice, and (2), which means to come out or go out. So, empty but not dead, empty but still producing even though dead, creation *ex nihilo*.

Yang and Yin work that field like two hands working a bellows. *T'o* (3), or bellows, has as its first meaning a bag or sack open at both ends, an image of absurdity. What good is a sack open at both ends? The two holes are present in the character itself, strangely reminiscent of the woman of my dream who has not only the vaginal hole, but also a hole in her chest. Analyzed, the character disassembles into a bizarre assortment combining the mineral, vegetable, and animal realms. It suggests the medieval western notion of human soul as subsuming within itself animal and vegetable soul (soul was not extended to the inorganic realms though planets and stars were thought of as besouled). *Mu* (4), is wood or tree; *shih* (5), is stone or mineral; *ch'ung* (6), is worms, insects, or reptiles. The image combines to suggest something very primitive yet cosmic about soul. It is nothing and yet everything. The sack open at both ends does in fact have a use when it is worked by Heaven and Earth. It puffs and blows and

1. 尸   a corpse or one who impersonates the dead ancestors at a sacrifice.

2. 出   come out or go out.

3. 橐   t'o—bellows. (Chinese)

4. 木   mu—wood or tree. (Chinese)

5. 石   shih—stone or mineral. (Chinese)

6. 虫   ch'ung—worms, insects, or reptiles. (Chinese)

feeds the flame (of spirit?). It also makes music as it blows. The character *yo* (1), which I have translated rather awkwardly as "plays/blows," refers to an ancient kind of flute, perhaps a sort of panpipe, with three or six holes. The exhalations of soul are not only practical, like the bellows, but playful like the flute. Soul is an essentially musical reality (or unreality).

Oddly enough, the image of no soul (the hole in her chest, a sack open at both ends) is the very possibility of soul. In our own language 'bellows' refers not only to the practical device which feeds air to flame, but to the pipe organ, the accordion, the lungs, even to the belly and the womb, to bulls and elephants, cannons and thunder. Taken back to the mystical realm of the root, *bhel-* means to blow and swell (sexual swollenness, all round objects, stones, bowls, fools, and bawds), to thrive and bloom (to foliate, flower, blossom, bloom, and blade), to cry out or yell (to bell, bellow, belch, or bawl), to shine, flash, or burn in bright colors or white hot or cold (blue, bleach, bleak, blaze, blemish, blind, blink, blank, blanch, blush, blaze, black, flame, phlegm). It is both the cry and the flash of soul as it suffers the Gods, whether it will or no. Gilgamesh can no more escape the Goddess than modern woman can free herself of the God. In the struggle with and against there is soul-making. Air to Flame.

4

And Simeon blessed them, and said unto Mary his mother, Behold, this child is set for the fall and rising again of many in Israel;
And for a sign which shall be spoken against;
(Yea, a sword shall pierce through thy own soul also,)
That the thoughts of many hearts may be revealed. (Luke 2:34–35)

Why is her Passion placed in parentheses? Is it a mere aside? "And, by the way . . . lest I forget." Is there something about her suffering which makes it almost unnoticeable? Something which could be over-

---

1. 籥   yo—plays/blows, as on an ancient flute or panpipe. (Chinese)

looked more easily than not, more readily than not? Is it but the background to the foreground of his drama? Or is it not the very ground of his drama? What but the MATERiality of this sign makes it unacceptable?

Is the parenthesis there to make clear that it is not her Passion which reveals the thoughts of hearts? It is true, is it not, that her condition does not impel us to consciousness? It is not a stone of stumbling or a rock of offense which, if we do not trip over it, falls upon us to crush. Even women, the very ones who suffer the sword thrust or the cannon blast, are slow to realize that something has gone wrong. It is like some bullet wounds which make only a tiny hole at the point of entry. You have to look on the underside of reality to discover the ravages. But what would provoke you to look?

The parenthesis describes the hole. It is like a hole in thought, a hole in the revelation. And yet the revelation is addressed to her, the bearer of the hole. Perhaps it takes a hole to receive a revelation, to bear it. "Thirty spokes make a wheel/ It turns on the center hole," says Lao Tzu (#11). Is there something missing in the revelation? Is it necessarily missing? Is what is not there as much a part of the revelation as what is? Is it perhaps the key? The old prophet is speaking. He has waited all his life for this moment. He is making his solemn utterance. God speaks through him. Something interrupts his train of thought. A distraction? A divergence from his theme? Who or what intrudes upon such a moment? Is there something about the attentive silence of the addressee?

The center hole, is it too a sign which shall be spoken against? No, there is nothing to protest, is there? It evokes a different reaction: a hiccup in the thought process, a momentary blank, a hesitation, a sudden chill, a sweat, a sharp intake of breath, perhaps a Freudian slip of the tongue. What happened? Who knows? Thought falters before the presentiment of an abyss. We want to rush away from such a moment not daring to look back, our hearts galloping faster than our legs. We feel a desperate need to recover ourselves. From what? Where did our selves go in that momentary lapse? But the aged prophet is able to continue speaking (where does he find the heart for it?); he utters the abyss itself (what language does he speak?). "Yea ..." he affirms it, "a sword shall pierce through thy own soul also."

So she has a soul after all. A soul with a hole in it, or a soul which is that hole. She herself declares it: "My soul doth magnify the Lord ..." (Lk. 1:46). To magnify is to make greater in size; to enlarge; to amplify; to intensify; to heighten. Is her soul such that it can add to

God? How can that be? Is it because of the hole? Is there something about a hole which enlarges, amplifies, intensifies, or heightens? Lao Tzu says that all things come from Being, but Being (*yu*, 1) comes from Non-Being (*wu*, 2) (#40). In the West through a marriage of Hebrew religion and Greek philosophy, God has come to be identified with Being. "And God said unto Moses, I AM THAT I AM: and he said, 'Thus shalt thou say unto the children of Israel, I AM hath sent me unto you' " (Ex. 3:14). "Jesus said unto them, Verily, verily, I say unto you, Before Abraham was, I am" (Jn. 8:58). In the West, Being is ultimate; in the East, Being is penultimate. Beyond Being is Non-Being. Beyond God is Soul.

To western sensibilities such a claim smacks of sheer blasphemy on the one hand, philosophical nonsense on the other. But suppose we give the eastern point of view a hearing before dismissing it altogether? There may be something there to help us through our own existential dilemmas and out of our psychological one-sidedness. First, how do they imagine Being, the source of all things? The character *yu* (3) in its primitive form shows a hand (4) reaching for a piece of meat (5). In the old days when a pupil first presented himself before a teacher, he always brought an offering. The humblest offering was a little dried meat wrapped up. It corresponds to our minimal notion of being as anything at all insofar as it is, being as the least common denominator of all things. It does not take too much imagination, however to see the primitive character (6) as a hand reaching for a penis, also known as "a piece," "a piece of meat." The seemingly endless stream of linguistic epithets for the genitalia—male and female—points to a *fascinosum* which might by contrast be called a

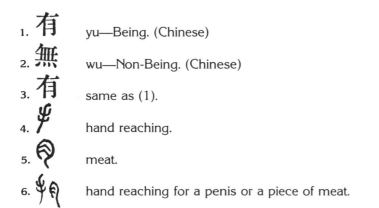

1. 有 yu—Being. (Chinese)

2. 無 wu—Non-Being. (Chinese)

3. 有 same as (1).

4.   hand reaching.

5.   meat.

6.   hand reaching for a penis or a piece of meat.

maximal notion of Being (and Non-Being). Certainly the penis is an apt image for the generative power. Later, the character evolves (whether poetically or euphemistically) into a hand reaching for the moon (1), and is finally abbreviated to (2). The moon is the mysterious source of the dew which refreshes the earth at night, and is the controller of all fluids (the tides, menses, etc.). Why should it not be the mystical source of soma and semen, the secret essence? Is that what we mean by "the Man in the Moon"? To lay hold of the secret essence is to be or to have (*yu* means both being and having); from the secret essence all things are engendered.

Wu (3) comes from the radical (4) meaning "tree." It shows an overgrown forest (5), here abbreviated to (6) with fire burning below (7) or (8) to indicate "the clearing after a forest fire."[13] Early methods of hunting by burning huge stretches of savannah or forest must have brought about the discovery that grasses and plants grow back better and healthier than ever after the destruction. In this event early man contemplated a mystery: Being comes from Non-Being. *Yu* has its source in *Wu*. The English correlate to *wu* would have to be 'nought', which by contrast to the image of a clearing carries no hint of positive potentiality, except through the mathematical functions and mystical overtones of its secondary meanings as the numeral zero (not intro- duced into western consciousness until the 13th century A.D.) and the figure 0. In its primary meaning 'nought' is "no +*wiht*," which further broken down to "*ne* + $\bar{a}$ + wight" means not ever the smallest thing or creature, or as "*ne* + $\bar{a}$ + whit" means not ever the least bit, particle

1. 𣏟   hand reaching for the moon.

2. 有   abbreviated form of (1).

3. 無   wu—Non-Being. (Chinese)

4. 木   tree (radical form).

5. 森   overgrown forest.

6. 無   abbreviated form of (5).

7. 灬   fire burning or

8. ⌒⌒   the clearing after a forest fire.

or iota, while the word 'naughty', which once meant "wicked, evil, or worthless," is now used only of children's misdeeds and of playful forms of sexual indecency. In terms of current usage or, psychologically speaking, in terms of what is functioning at an explicitly conscious level, 'nought' or 'naught' has been rendered all but obsolete, while 'naughty' has been trivialized.

The secondary meanings do reverberate in our unconscious if not in our consciousness, however. In fact, to the degree that they slip from consciousness, they loom and proliferate in the unconscious mind. The negative and negated etymon flips over to the secretly affirmative and secretly affirmed symbolon. As in algebra, a negated negative equals an affirmative. Significantly, it was shortly after the introduction of zero, which in Sanskrit (*sunya*) and in Arabic (*aṣ-ṣifr*) means "empty," toward the end of the 13th and the beginning of the 14th centuries, that Meister Eckhart began preaching the "noughting" of God and the soul.[14] *Nihtes niht* is the Middle High German term he coined to express (1) what the soul is in itself: "All creatures are mere nothingness. I do not say that they are small or anything at all: they are mere nothingness" (Sermon "Every good gift"); (2) what the soul is apart from God: "Outside of God there is nothing but only nothingness" (Sermon "One God and Father of all"); (3) what God is in himself: "When he saw nothing, he saw God" (Sermon "Saul rose from the ground"); (4) what the soul is in God: "When I cease projecting myself into any image, when no image is represented any longer in me, and when I cast out of myself whatever is in me, then I am ready to be transported into the naked being of God" (Sermon "See what love").

The complement of *nihtes niht* is *ihtes iht,* "this individual being" or "this something". He uses *ihtes iht* to express (1) what God is to the soul: "When the mind penetrates into the unmixed light, it falls into its non-being (*nihtes niht*), and it is so far removed in this non-being from its created something (*iht*) that its own powers are incapable of bringing it back into its created something. So God places his uncreated being under the mind's non-being (*nihtes niht*) and maintains the mind with his something (*iht-es iht*)" (Sermon "Jesus went into the temple"); (2) what the soul is to God: "And if I myself were not, God would not be either: That God is God, of this I am a cause. If I were not, God would not be God" (Sermon "Blessed are the poor").[15] Neither Eckhart nor Lao Tzu denies the reality and importance of Being, but in both the inclination is toward Non-Being. They are thinkers in the feminine mode, under the aegis of soul. They are both aware that the negative cannot be thought except in relation to the positive, but, unlike some thinkers of Being, they are also fully aware that the positive cannot be thought except in relation to the negative. Their genius consists in the inflection they give to the negative. They operate "from within the hole."

If we push the analysis of 'nought' further, down to the level of meaning carried by the sounds themselves, we have to ask what is the meaning of 'n'? The Greek form *nu* comes from a Phoenician word meaning "fish", earlier "snake" (which is borne out by the earliest written form of the letter (1)). In Hebrew snake is *nachash,* in Sanskrit *naga.* Fundamentally it is the same word, the same sound, even though Hebrew and Sanskrit are ancient forms of supposedly unrelated language families. As we move farther back and into deeper levels of what is today for the most part a profoundly unconscious resonance of language, the emphasis shifts from the contents of the unconscious (fish) to the underlying power of the unconscious (snake), which corresponds better to the archaic Semitic root *nyn* meaning "to increase" or, possibly, "to endure". My soul (*nephesh*) magnifies, increases, enlarges, amplifies, intensifies, heightens, and makes enduring ... the Lord.

Perhaps it is just a coincidence, but the word for woman in many language families turns on the "n" sound, as does the name of the Goddess Inanna. The written character for the Chinese *nü* (2), meaning "woman," emphasizes the hole in the middle. It looks like a woman walking with her arms stretched out wide, baring and bearing the central hole. The older form of the character is more sinuous (3) with an emphasis on the hips and the right arm pointing to the genital region. Even so, there is a beginning awareness of the hole in the upper region, a repetition of the birth cavity at a higher level, whereas the earliest form (4) concentrates attention on the physical cavity with no indication of an awareness of repetition at the psychic level. Our own language

1. ７   nu—fish or snake (earliest written form). (Phoenician)

2. 女   nü—woman. (Chinese)

3. ㄈ   older form of (2).

4. ㄇ   earliest form of (2).

presents us with the image of a womb-man. Tracing back the syllable 'wo', we reach 'wife', and from there to 'wave', 'vivid', 'vibrant', 'vibrate', and at long last 'viper'. In relation to the 'n' sound we have 'nanny', but also nubile, nurse, nourish, and nymph.

The 'n' sound imitates the action of swallowing, whence the profound relation to nubility (having breasts) and nursing, and thus to flowing rivers (Hebrew *nahar*), naiads, and navies. The cursive forms of 43c and 43d imitate the waves of the ocean. These waves are, I believe, the secret of the power in many mantric sounds, most of which end in 'm' or 'n' and tend, when prolonged, to set up vibrations which are conducive to trance. They lead into the unconscious which is a kind of night (*nihtes niht;* Greek *nux*), but also a light (Hebrew *ner,* candle; Arabic *nur,* light; Greek *nous,* mind). They lead into that hole which looks like lack of soul, inferiority, nothing doing, but from which everything springs, even God.

5

In the formative years of Christianity there was some controversy over whether or not Christ had really died on the cross. It is probably the factual reason behind the solemn testimony given by the apostle John to the sure sign of death when Jesus' side is pierced by the soldier's spear (Jn. 19:34−37). Soldiers had been dispatched to hasten the death of the crucified men by breaking their legs, which would induce suffocation. When they came to Jesus they saw that he was already dead so they did not break his legs, mysteriously fulfilling a prophecy regarding the Paschal Lamb, "a bone of him shall not be broken" (Jn. 19:36; cf. Ex. 12:46; Ps. 34:20). And so he did not die through loss of breath (prana, chi, ki, energy, pneuma, psyche), but rather gave up his spirit voluntarily with a great cry (Mt. 27:50; Mk. 15:37; Lk. 23:46). The wound to the chest area does not cause death either since he is observed to be dead already, but gives as it were the sure sign of the aftermath of death, the outpouring of blood and water. "But one of the soldiers with a spear pierced his side, and forthwith came there out blood and water" (Jn. 19:34). When I first began thinking

1. *m* cursive form of "m". (Roman)

2. *n* cursive form of "n". (Roman)

about the dream of the woman with the hole in her chest, my thoughts were drawn to the sacred wounds of Christ and in particular to the Great Wound in his side. I thought there might be some connection or some possibility of mutual illumination between the woman's wound and the wound to Christ's side, even though her chest is blasted away and his is pierced by a spear. As I now reread the scriptural texts I am especially struck by two points: one is that the chest wound does not cause death but shows the aftermath of death; the other is that John's solemn testimony serves psychologically to draw our attention not so much to the fact of death as to the opening and the outpouring which ensue.

Is there a sure sign of death? The question has new meaning in our time of organ transplants, near-death experiences, and debate over extraordinary measures to prolong human life. If we are not certain what exactly constitutes death, do we know how to recognize the aftermath of death? It seems to me that the showing to which John testifies in the Gospel is more of a revelation than it is a confirmation of something already known. Do we know that death is an opening and an outpouring? Can we who are on this side of death even begin to understand it? I believe that we can have some understanding of it by way of contemplation ("they shall look on him whom they pierced" [Jn. 19:37]) and by way of analogous experience. The two go together. We go through or have the opportunity to go through a number of "death and resurrection" experiences prior to our physical death. To have contemplated a revelation of the good side of death nourishes the faith required to let go of the previous life.

"They shall look on him whom they pierced" (Jn. 19:37). It is regarded by John as the fulfillment of the prophecy in Zechariah 12:10, which actually reads "and they shall look upon *me* whom they have pierced, and they shall mourn for *him*, as one mourneth for his only son." Even in the Hebrew text there is a mysterious identification between God and the one who is pierced. It is further reinforced by John who unifies in one symbol the sacrificial animal through which release from bondage is secured, a suffering God, and a humble human Messiah whose death provides access to the secret place, the heart or Holy of Holies, and to the fluids of eternal life. There is a curious ambivalence to the contemplation of the pierced heart however, depending upon whether it is viewed from without, as it is by those who have done the piercing (cf. Rev. 1:7), or from within, as it is by those for whom it is the paradigm of their own experience. In actuality we each belong to both groups, the victimizers and the victimized, whence the profound ambiguity of religious experience, producing both paroxysms of guilt and the bliss of salvation. In terms of psychological health the two poles of experiential insight must somehow be held together.

According to Jung, the only thing which can hold opposites together is the spontaneous emergence of what he calls the "transcendent function," a unifying symbol

which itself transcends time and conflict, neither adhering to nor partaking of one side or the other but somehow common to both and offering the possibility of a new synthesis. The word "transcendent" is expressive of the presence of a capacity to transcend the destructive tendency to pull (or be pulled) to one side or the other.[16]

The apostle John must have seen the gratuitous deed of the soldier, piercing and opening the heart of Christ, spilling and releasing the water and the blood as just such a reconciling symbol. It casts light backwards to a scene of Jesus teaching during a celebration of the Feast of Tabernacles:

In the last day, that great day of the feast, Jesus stood and cried, saying, "If any man thirst, let him come unto me, and drink. He that believeth on me, as the scripture hath said, out of his belly shall flow rivers of living water." (But this spake he of the Spirit, which they that believe on him should receive: for the Holy Ghost was not yet given; because that Jesus was not yet glorified.) (John 7:37–39)

In this very dense text there is a certain providential ambiguity arising from an uncertainty in the tradition as to whether the "his" of "his belly" (RSV: "heart"; NEB: "from within him") refers to Jesus or to the believer. The most likely answer is that it refers both ways so that to the Great Wound of Christ must correspond a similar wound in the believer, a wound, even a death wound, which is also a glorification as a baptism and communion in the Spirit. John would also have had in mind another text from Zechariah (14:8), which was used in the liturgy of the feast: "And it shall be in that day, that living waters shall go out from Jerusalem; half of them toward the former sea [the Dead Sea], and half of them toward the hinder sea [the Mediterranean]: in summer and winter shall it be." The living waters will revivify the Dead Sea and make a connection between the waters of the past and the waters of the future. They will flow continually, in the dry season as well as in the wet.

Psychologically, the sea is the unconscious. It is made up of salt water, closely akin to lifeblood, whereas the river, which flows backward and forward between past and future, is fresh water. The water is a living and life-giving connection between the blood sea of the past and the blood sea of the future. As fresh water, it both has the capacity for "freshening" (renewing, refertilizing, or making alive), and serves as a conscious connection at the feeling level between the forgotten past and the unknown future, the one feeding into the other by means of the fresh water. We experience a conflict between future and past, the conflict of generations, or the conflict between progressive and traditional civilizations, or an interior conflict of loyalties between that which gave us life and that towards which life calls. The living water, both salt and fresh, which flows from the heart chakra, heals that conflict in an unpredictable manner. It shows itself to be a source greater even than the sea of the past or the sea of the future—to be the source of all sources.

In his First Letter (5:6–8) John continues his reflections:

This is he that came by water and blood, even Jesus Christ; not by water only, but by water and blood. And it is the Spirit that beareth witness, because the Spirit is truth. For there are three that bear record (in heaven, the Father, the Word, and the Holy Ghost; and these three are one. And there are three that bear witness in earth,) the Spirit, and the water, and the blood: and these three agree in one.

The words inside the parenthesis seem to be a gloss introduced into later manuscripts of the Vulgate edition of the Bible. The gloss finds in the threesome a suggestion of the Christian doctrine of God as trinity in the form of an earthly trinity mirroring a heavenly trinity. For John the threesome (water, blood, and Spirit) fulfill a requirement of the Torah (Dt. 19:15; Nm. 35:30) that to make a case, particularly in a criminal proceeding, there must be at least two or three witnesses. In our case there are in one sense (outwardly) two witnesses, water and blood, and in another sense (inwardly) three witnesses, water, blood, and Spirit. The water and the blood are poured out by means of the death wound, plunged into through baptism (ritually through the sacrament, existentially through analogous experience) and imbibed through communion in the Spirit (ritually through the sacrament, existentially through understanding the experience). The testimony is received through a profound identification of Spirit between the believer and the Christ who releases the Spirit with a great cry (voluntarily).

The *point de touche* between the heavenly trinity and the earthly trinity is the commonality of Spirit. Would it be farfetched to say that while the heavenly trinity is masculine, the earthly trinity is feminine (the fluid realm being a female symbol), and Spirit is both male and female? The deeper sense of the *point de touche* is of course the connection between the reality of God and human reality, whether male or female, but for my purposes I want to notice the presence and significance of female reality in the Mystery. The *point de touche* occurs at the level of the heart chakra, in the soul realm and in that precise part or feature of soul (Eros) which is associated with the female. In this instance in contrast with Luke 2:35, it is the male Logos which is placed in parentheses.

If the first thousand years of Christianity focussed on Christ as Logos (the throat chakra), during the second thousand years the emphasis has shifted to Christ as Eros. It has been a shift inspired by the spiritual genius of women, beginning with Mechtild and Gertrude in the 13th century, Gertrude being called the prophet of devotion to the Sacred Heart of Jesus, and culminating in the efforts of Margaret Mary Alacoque in the 17th century to win official church approval and support of the cult. The devotion was approved in 1765 by Clement XIII with official doctrine proclaimed in the papal bull *Miserentissimus Redemptor* in 1928 and a special Mass and Office of the Sacred Heart approved by Pius XI in 1929.

There are aspects of the history of mystical devotion to the Sacred Heart which may strike us as frankly if not perversely erotic. Ludgarde (1182–1246) has a vision of the bleeding side wound, her heart united to his Heart; Ida (1243–1300) drinks from the Source. Gertrude (1256–1302) receives the stigmata, her heart pierced by a ray of light from the Sacred Heart. She places her hand into the Great Wound and draws it back wearing seven rings of gold. Margaret of Cortona (1247–1297) kisses the Wound, entering into the secrets of divine tenderness. Angela of Foligno (1246–1309) drinks blood from the Wound. The list goes on. Christ appears to Margaret Mary Alacoque, shows her his Heart, and asks for prayer and reparation. The eroticism of celibate women is displaced onto the person of Jesus as animus, but particularly when he is identified with the heart chakra. Could there be in all this a not quite conscious realization that God is to be found in the erotic as well as in the spiritual? Would the other side of reparation to the Sacred Heart for the sins of humankind be a divine redemption of Eros?

Two major differences between the Great Wound of Christ and the wound of the woman with the hole in her chest are, first, that her wound emphasizes only the opening, not the outpouring; second, that she is the bearer of the wound, not the animus. In the complex symbolism of the aftermath of death we might think of the opening as the yin moment of receptivity and the outpouring as the yang moment of creativity. It would make sense that there should be a female accentuation of the yin feature. In the transfer of the wound from the male figure to the female there may be a partial owning of her own soul, not yet complete since she cannot identify with the outpouring. If one of the more terrible aspects of the Goddess is that she brings death to her lovers, here there would be some realization or a foretelling of a realization that it is her own soul which is desirous of death. "But I have a baptism to be baptised with; and how am I straightened till it be accomplished" (Lk. 12:50). In the death desire there is not necessarily a morbidity or a failure to savor the good things of life, but an awareness, however dim, that the soul's fulfillment lies on the other side.

Endnotes

1. Why is it that, when someone's genitals are exposed, the first reaction is to laugh?
2. The connection is hinted at by the Yahwist author of Genesis 3 by means of a pun between 'naked' (*arummim*) and 'subtil' (*arum*).
3. The story is included in Diane Wolkstein and Samuel Noah Kramer, *Inanna: Queen of Heaven and Earth: Her Stories and Hymns from Sumer* (New York: Harper and Row, 1983).
4. See, for instance, St. Thomas Aquinas, *Summa Theologiae,* la. 92, 1: "Should woman have been made in that original creation of things?", objs. 1 and 2 with the replies.
5. Cf. Ps. 74:5−6.
6. The Sumerian depiction of the *Anzu*-bird with an eagle body and a lion head strikes me as a patriarchal metamorphosis, as is the King James rendition of Mt. 24:28, where the sign of the Second Coming is "For wheresoever the carcase is, there will the eagles be gathered together," whereas the sense of the text demands a gathering of vultures.
7. The legend may be found in Robert Graves and Raphael Patai, *Hebrew Myths* (New York: Greenwich House, 1963), pp. 65−69.
8. N. K. Sandars, trans., *Epic of Gilgamesh* (London: Penguin, 1960), pp. 85−87.
9. Inanna had first called upon her divine brother, Utu, to cut down the Tree. Utu, who is the sun (full consciousness), did refuse, but full consciousness is a divine prerogative, not a human possibility.
10. Sandars, *Gilgamesh,* p 88.
11. Cf. Manfred Lurker, *The Gods and Symbols of Ancient Egypt* (New York: Thames and Hudson, 1980), under "National Shrine," p. 84.
12. I owe this interpretation to Hugh A. Moran, *The Alphabet and Ancient Calendar Signs* (Palo Alto, Cal.: Pacific Books, 1953), p. 45.
13. See Chungliang Al Huang's *Quantum Soup* (New York: Dutton, 1983), p. 92 for this interpretation.
14. Eckhart does have predecessors in the West, chiefly PseudoDionysos (6th c.), who speaks of being and super-being, and John Scotus Erigena (9th c.), who plays with the notions of created and uncreated as modalities of nature.
15. All citations are from Reiner Schurmann, *Meister Eckhart: Mystic and Philosopher* (Bloomington, Ind.: Indiana University Press, 1978). See Schurmann's discussion of *nihtes niht* and *ihtes iht* on pp. 85−92.
16. A. Samuels, B. Shorter and F. Plant, *A Critical Dictionary of Jungian Analysis* (London: Routledge and Kegan Paul, 1986), p. 150.

Chapter Two

Is This It?

At least part of the reason why Jung was fascinated with the medieval question *Habet mulier animam?* is that it leads into one of his principal theories, that of the contrasexual character of the soul. Accordingly, he answers the question, *Mulier non habet animam, sed animum.*[1] Woman does not have an anima, as does a man; she has an animus. If outwardly (as embodied) we are of a determinate, and thus limited gender, inwardly (as besouled) there is a complementary opposite which we need and instinctively seek to round out our humanity. Basic to the theory is the belief that humanity is something "round," a fullness, a whole world which is at once unique, for there are any number of variations on the theme and "thisness" is never fully overcome (this not that, now not then, here not there), and universal, for there is a theme, a common story of grandeur and misery (thou art that).

There are differences, however, between the ways a man relates to his inwardness and the ways a woman relates to hers. Jung claims that a man has ordinarily a quite specific image of the anima; it gives a focus to his quest. Its very specificity may make it more available to consciousness, though it will baffle consciousness so long as there is a blurred distinction between 'it' (the anima as an inner component of the man's reality and as a transcendent factor) and 'she' (a flesh-and-blood woman on whom the anima is projected). The anima is an essential part of a man's world; a real woman is another world. So for a woman the animus is an inner component of her world as well as a guide to the transcendent, while a real man is another world. All other people are other worlds and there is a need for these worlds to intersect, but that is another, though related story.

33

While the man may have a clear image, if not a clear under-standing, of the anima, Jung relates that he has "as a rule, found it very difficult to make a woman understand what the animus is, and I have never met any woman who could tell me anything definite about his personality."[2] So in my dream the woman with the hole in her chest moves into the arms of her lover and is instantly healed, though all that she can see of him is his hands and forearms. Why is she unable to see him clearly? And what does it mean for her relationship to her own soul?

There is a famous story, which like most truly great stories appears in many forms all over the world, about Soul and her relationship to her Lover. But already a problem presents itself. It is a question which has been lurking in the background from the beginning of my inquiry, the unspoken half of the *Habet mulier animam?* Does woman have a soul? Or is she Soul? And if she is Soul, who is her ghostly Lover? Or is it a mistake for a flesh-and-blood woman to slip into the role of Soul, a confused response to the male bafflement between 'it' and 'she'? In one form or another, the problem has been pondered by the best theological and philosophical minds of East and West for many centuries now, and the considered answer seems to be "yes and no."

Aware of the question, if unable to answer it, let us turn to the story which will give us the best and most farreaching orientation to-wards the questions raised. As Plato was wont to say, it is "only a story," but one which comes closer to Truth than all our reasonings.[3]

In an early Greek form of the story she is not yet called Soul. She is clearly a woman, the daughter of Cadmus of Thebes, and her name is Semele, which probably means "earth" (from a Thracian word *zemelo*). Zeus fell in love with her and came to her disguised as a man. When she was already six months pregnant, jealous Hera under the guise of an old neighbor woman planted a seed of doubt, curiosity, anxiety, jealousy and/or suspicion in Semele's ear. What about Zeus's disguise? Is Semele missing something? What is his true form? How did he appear to Hera when he courted her? Or is he in disguise because he has something to hide? What if he is some sort of monster? The seed grew and did its work. First she begged, finally she insisted that Zeus reveal himself. Either because he had once promised to grant her every wish or angered by her nagging, he showed her his glory and she was blasted by lightning. Zeus snatched his unborn son from the fire and sewed him up in his own thigh where he matured a further three months and came forth Dionysos, the "twice-born." Later, after he had established himself in his Godhood, Dionysos went down to the underworld to obtain his mother's release by a gift of myrtle to Persephone, and brought her with him into heaven.

I say she is "clearly a woman," and the gist of the story demands that she be so, as Walter Otto argues so well.[4] The mystery on which the story turns is how two such disparate realities, the human and the divine, could come together in love. The story seems to say that they cannot do so, that the weaker term is annihilated in the encounter. Or it says that they can come together, but only if the stronger term of the relationship hides itself and if the weaker term will be content with a symbol. It seems to me that the story casts some light on why woman has no vision of the animus, or why that vision is unfocussed, multiple, and diffuse.[5]

There is a touching innocence about the beginning of the relationship. She does not overreach herself or set her sights too high. It is the God who comes to her. The story does not tell us just how he presented himself to her, except that it was in the form of a man. However he was, she found him attractive. They became lovers; she was carrying his child. Then Hera enters on the scene, also in disguise as the older, wiser woman. Semele's heart must not belong entirely to her lover because there is some part of her which listens to Hera. In the end Hera's voice prevails over her lover's voice; thus Semele's downfall. How could such a thing happen?

Did Semele know that her lover was Zeus before Hera arrived, or was it Hera who sprung the surprise? What we know is that Hera emphasized, underlined, emblazoned on Semele's mind the fact of the disguise. "You have never seen your lover the way he really is; if only you could see what is beneath the mask ..." So Hera might have spoken. Hera is wise enough in the ways of love to know that love wants to know the beloved as thoroughly as possible, or more than possible. Love resents that there may be some part of the beloved, some detail of his past, an adventure, a suffering which she has not shared. What will she do if she discovers that what she does know of him is not what he really is? Does it mean that the relationship is founded on untruth? Has he deceived her by coming in disguise?

The old neighbor woman plays on the extremes of possibility. On the one hand, she insinuates that Semele has no idea of his true beauty. If only she could see him as he was when he courted Hera ... Is there something which Hera knows and enjoys but which Semele can never have? Is she to be admitted to the outer court of his love but never to the innermost sanctuary of his being? On the other hand, would any honest person refuse to show himself? If he insists on a disguise, is it not because he has something shameful (or terrible) to hide? And what can Semele be thinking of to surrender herself to she knows not what?

Surely Zeus tried to reason with her, but how could he have explained to her in such a way that she could understand? And once the urgency of her need to rip away the veil was aggravated to such a pitch, what could have tempered it? What shall we say of this desire to see which outstrips all human possibility? Semele's desire is born of ignorance and mixed with all sorts of impurities, which must have caused great grief to her lover. There is unlove mixed with her love; what can he do about that? He may appeal to their love and to the happiness they have shared, but she will no longer hear of it. That is all in question now. What she does know of him is suspended in thin air, surrounded as it is by the awful darkness of what has been hidden from her.

And so she insists upon seeing what no one can see and live. Her story shows us that there is a difference between the desire to see and the desire for God. God she had and in such tenderness and intimacy that even Hera was rendered jealous. Is it not strange that Hera should be filled with such murderous hate towards a mortal woman, she who is equal in divinity to Zeus, who can bear the full brunt of his being, who enjoys the privileges of the legitimate wife? Is it possible that the opposite of her insinuation is the real truth, that Semele knows and enjoys something which Hera can never have? But there is a condition to Semele's continued possession of that knowledge and that joy. It is a hard condition, perhaps the hardest of all, not to see. Not to have her doubts, her curiosity, her anxiety, her jealousy, her suspicions laid to rest by a showing. To have to find a way herself to lay them to rest unanswered. The condition proves too hard for Semele, or perhaps it does not occur to her that it is her task, not his.

In a Latin version of the story, as told by Apuleius in *The Golden Ass,* she is called Psyche. She is the youngest of three daughters born to royal parents in an unnamed kingdom. All three daughters are beautiful but Psyche far outshines her elder sisters, so much so that the people want to worship her as a goddess, so much so that no young man dares court her. She is said to be more beautiful than Aphrodite, a dangerous thing to say even if it is true, for when the rumor reaches Aphrodite's ear, she falls into a dark rage. Aphrodite conceives a plan; she sends her son, Eros, to afflict Psyche by making her fall in love with a man of no worth. Meanwhile, Psyche's parents have consulted the oracle of Apollo to find a suitable marriage partner for her. They are told to leave her on a high mountain where she must wed a serpentine monster of which even Zeus and the Styx are afraid. Psyche's parents are crushed with sorrow but cannot disobey the oracle. Psyche tries to comfort them, taking the blame herself for not putting a stop to all that foolish "goddess" worship.

Somehow Semele had threatened the divine marriage, the union of male and female in the Godhead. It was simultaneously a threat to the human institution of marriage as ultimate value. Here came a new, heretofore unheard-of possibility, a union of the divine and the human. Is it unthinkable? Psyche threatens the godlike status of romantic love by possessing a beauty and a desireableness which are even fairer than Aphrodite. Is it unimaginable?

Eros, however, would not carry out his mother's revenge. He himself was conquered by Psyche's beauty. He commanded the West Wind to bear her away from the mountaintop to a castle he had prepared for her. There every good thing was placed at her disposal; she found herself in a garden of delights. At night her lover would come to her unseen. It is said that she knew him only by touch and hearing, but what she learned through those two senses caused her to fall deeply, passionately in love.

After a time her lover, whose name she did not know, warned her that her sisters would try to find her. Excited by the news, for it had been a long time since she had seen anyone, she begged for a chance to visit with them. On the first visit they were stunned by her good fortune. Their own lives seemed bleak and miserable by comparison. Their hearts turned; how could they bear for Psyche to have so much and they so little? More time passed and her lover warned Psyche that her sisters would return. Again she begged to see them. Though he warned her specifically that they would urge her to look at his face, she would not believe that they were her enemies. Nor was she deterred when he promised that the child she was carrying would be born divine if she kept the secret, but mortal if she divulged it.

Why this jealousy of heaven and earth? Why should immortals like Hera and Aphrodite resent a human participation in their prerogatives? Why do Psyche's sisters, who had shuddered at her fate, resent their own lives when they discover her well and happy? Why do heaven and earth conspire to destroy soul? What are her chances, caught as she is between forces determined to tear her apart, to keep heaven and earth forever separate and unmingled?

And what of her child? Semele's child is a God despite her fall from grace. Or perhaps because of her fall from grace? Did he become

God in the divine fire? Or was it because Zeus bore him in and from his own thigh? Or was he perhaps two parts man from the six months he spent in Semele's womb and one part God from the three months he spent with Zeus? However it may be, he had to struggle to establish his divinity. The fate of Psyche's child hangs in the balance. In her case it is clear that the woman has a critical role to play in determining the essential being of the child. How strange it is—while the child could not be divine if it were not the child of Eros, that much we understand, it cannot be divine without the work, the suffering, and the faithfulness of Psyche. This we do not understand.

Psyche invented stories about her lover to ward off the volley of questions her sisters never tired of firing at her. But before long she caught herself in a contradiction and then the sisters knew that she had never actually seen him. They pounced on their opportunity like hungry tigresses. They reminded Psyche that according to the oracle, which may not be disputed, she was to marry a snake. It was too horrible to contemplate. Then they told her what to do: how she must conceal a lamp and a sharp knife and, when her lover had fallen into a deep sleep, how she must take the lamp so that she could see what she was doing and plunge the knife into his neck.

Believing them (and at a deeper level believing the oracle), yet torn between the love she still felt and her terror of what came to her in the dark, Psyche did as she was told. When Eros fell asleep that night, her sisters having departed in haste, she took the lamp from its hiding place and seized the knife. And then she saw. She stood there rapt, gazing at the wondrous beauty of the God, when a drop of hot oil from the lamp fell on his shoulder, waking him. He opened his eyes, saw at a glance what had happened, spread his great wings, and left her.

Who suffers the worst fate, Psyche or Semele? While the consequences for Semele were more drastic, her pain and her realization were but a momentary flash. Psyche is not allowed to die. She must wander the earth stricken, inconsolable, unable to forget what she had had and what she had lost. Does she escape the great injunction? Does she see God and live? Would not that wondrous sight—how she strives to remember it now—so quickly gone, linger sufficiently in her memory to blight and dim all else? Can her miserable wanderings be called life? As Kierkegaard described the condition we call despair, she is sick unto death yet unable to die. Hers is a living death, unless there be for her some hope of redemption.

Apuleius has Aphrodite impose on Psyche what would ordinarily be considered four impossible tasks: she must sort out a huge heap of seeds before nightfall; she must bring a hank of golden wool from killer sheep; she must bring a vessel of water from the river Styx; she must bring Aphrodite a box of cosmetics from Persephone in the underworld. It is not clear from the story whether the accomplishment of these tasks would amount to a redemption. Certainly Aphrodite does not intend them as such. In each instance her purpose is to destroy Psyche. The tasks have then an ever increasing degree of difficulty and inherent danger.

Meanwhile Psyche is suicidal, not only by reason of unassuageable grief over her great loss, but also in face of the impossibility of the four tasks. In each instance, when she is at her wit's end, something outside her control comes to her assistance. First she must learn how to sort out the unsortable. What would that be but the multitudinous factors that come to bear at every moment of human life? It cannot be done consciously, but it can be done by the tiny ants which come to her aid. Both the English 'ant' and its Latin equivalent *formica* come from roots meaning "to bite" or "to cut." The fact that these cutters are insects, at a far remove from a human level of being, is an indication that her powers of discernment, powers able to deal with the enormous complexity of life, arise out of profoundly unconscious processes, a kind of Tao deeply embedded in the body like a subterranean river. She must reach down to the remote depths of her body knowledge, to what her body knows because it is part and parcel of all bodies to the farthest reaches of the universe. The mind must learn what the body already knows; body must become mind. Mind must become minding, paying attention to the tiniest stirrings, the movements of the ants.

Her second task is to gather golden wool from killer sheep. The image of killer sheep seems incongruous at first, until we think about the movements of mass psychology or of our own instincts. She must find the gold (the good) in what at an instinctual or semi-conscious level has the power to destroy her. Here she is assisted by a green reed which speaks to her, teaching her how to wait for the right moment when the sheep are lulled by an afternoon nap, and how to accomplish things indirectly by gathering the tufts of wool which cling to the briars instead of approaching the sheep directly. To be able to follow the voice of the reed she must have developed an unusual capacity for listening. She is able to understand the language of the birds and the trees, and of all the elements. It is said that she knew her lover by touch and by hearing, but not by sight. Her desire to know him coupled with her inability to see must have prompted an extraordinary refinement of her sense of touch and feeling and of her ability to listen. How alive she must have been to his least movement and to the merest whisper of his voice!

But what is it that she feels and hears? Who or what is this mysterious Eros? In ancient times it was believed that to know the name is to have hold of the essence of a being. Even so, our best clue to the being of Eros is in the name itself, the core of which is the 'r', which in its earliest Semitic form 𐤓 (*rēsh*) meant "head." A woman's inner task is to find her head, her true mind, as a man's inner task is to find his heart. Finding her true mind includes but goes beyond having a mind of her own, which may be mere opinionatedness. Jung describes the uncultivated animus as opinionatedness, while the uncultivated anima of the man is moodiness. Both opinionatedness and moodiness have a way of possessing the person, eclipsing one's humanity like an evil spell. One of Semele's sisters was called Autonoë ("with a mind of her own"). After Semele's death her sisters derided her memory by saying that she had lied in claiming her lover was Zeus and had been struck by lightning as punishment for her blasphemy. Dionysos avenged his mother and himself by afflicting all the women of Thebes with madness. In her maenadic frenzy Agave, another of the sisters, tore her own son limb from limb and devoured him.

To get some concrete idea of where her true mind might be found and how it would function, we need to go beyond the letter 'r', written language being a relative latecomer and addressed to the eye, to the 'r' sound and to the wealth of meaning which has been spun out of and around that sound over countless ages. 'Erh' is the sound made by a swiftly flowing river, and because rivers flow from the earth, the earth is Er or Rhea, the mother of the Gods, whose name, according to Chrysippus, comes from the Greek *rheo,* "I flow." Already we are given a sense of direction. Her mind ARises out of her EARth, hER body awAReness, and it flows like a RivER along a winding cOURse in sEARch of the sea. ERos is the active principle within her; without that flow and pulse she would be inERt. Her mind arises, ERupts from her gRound. What comes "from above" is fOReign to her unless, like the Rain, it agRees with what emERges from below in RHythm and in RHyme as from an ORacle. She enjoys the Riddle of existence. A wORd need not be logical in ORder to the tRue, but it must be EARnest, it must come from the hEARt and speak to the heart, and it must have a kind of fit, a hARmony. Things ARe insofAR as they are intERwoven with the whole. The totality is what she has a feel fOR. She REAds the REAsons of things in tERms of their ARt, how they wORk togethER.

Psyche's third task is to fetch a vessel of watER from the sOURce of the Styx, the river which forms a boundary between this life and the next. Only the dead can cross these waters; to touch them is to die. An eagle, the old English name for which is *ERne* (Greek *ORnis*), comes to her assistance flying over the waters, zig-zagging between dragons, and filling her cup. Eros is then a power of transcendence within her, something which reaches beyond the confines of mortality. Rendered accessible, the waters of death are transformed into living water, the promise of a greater life, one no longer bounded by the limitations of the flesh. Her true mind, proceeding as it does through the modes of touch and hEARing, has a capacity not just for relative truth (the more or less true; true within a particular frame of reference) but for Truth.

Her final task is to go down to the underworld to PERsephone to ask for a pORtion of her beauty to take in a box back to Aphrodite. In despAIR she decides to throw herself from a high tower, but the tower (Latin *tURris*), symbol of female introversion, instructs her care-fully on what she must do and not do in order to accomplish this most difficult mission safely. In the course of her jOURney she must lEARn to overcome false compassion, steeling her heart against the many demands made on it which would deflect her from her true pURpose, while meeting the rightful demands. Which is right for her and which is wrong she learns from the tower, the voice of her introvERsion. Most important, she is wARned not to open or even look at the precious box she carries, for "that hidden receptacle of divine beauty is not for you to explore." Psyche succeeds through every phase of her journey until the last when she succumbs to a desIRe to see what is inside the box.

It strains belief to imagine that Psyche, having suffered the loss of her great love by striving to see the forbidden, would commit the same mistake twice—and for a box of cosmetics. I conclude then that instead of a double mistake, it is the same mistake told in two different ways. The story of the four tasks is a retelling of the initial story at an inner level, in terms of Psyche's development. Eros appears in the retelling not as another person, a lover, but as the dynamism of her being, that from which and toward which she moves. Even the fatal desIRe to see comes from him (Eros is usually translated "desire"), though 'desire' means "away from the stAR," and so there is a paradox at work. Her desire causes her to lose her heart's desire.

What happens is that when Psyche opens the box, it appears to be empty. She sees nothing, but she falls into a deep, drugged sleep.

If it is true that the story of the tasks is a recapitulation, the inside of the outer story, then Psyche's sorrowful wanderings are a kind of sleep-walking. It is a bad dream from which she cannot awake until and unless her lover returns to her. But when he returns there is something she must do which amounts to a pURgation of the seeing faculty. In his return and in her learning to see without seeing lies her redemption.

For the story of her redemption, which on the face of it is a redemption of Eros, we must turn to "Beauty and the Beast." Psyche's sisters had reminded her of the oracle:

> Nec speres generum mortali stirpe creatum,
> Sed saevum atque ferum vipereumque malum,[6]

convincing her that what entered her bed by night was a great snake which would devour her and her child. If the oracle has spoken, it must indeed be true that Eros is none other than the ancient serpent, whom we have met in the Garden of Eden and beneath Inanna's tree. But by listening closely to the tales we also learn that the serpent is but one form, the chthonic form, of what can also appear as a lightning bolt or as a God of irresistible beauty. Perhaps it is Psyche's doubt, the rupturing of their troth, which fixes Eros in the form of Beast as though he were under an evil spell. She suspects him of being a monster and so she sees him as a monster. What she sees (or how she sees) is dictated by her heart.

Later, as Beauty, it is through the misfortunes of her father that she once again finds her lover. Beauty's father was a rich merchant who lost his fortune when a ship carrying all his goods was wrecked at sea. The family, consisting of three sons and three daughters, the mother being long dead, had to move to a modest country place and live like rustics. Beauty, the youngest of the three daughters, was sensitive to her father's plight and put the best possible face on things, throwing herself into the farm chores with good will. Her sisters meanwhile sulked and complained and longed only for city life. Word came that the shipwreck had washed ashore and all were excited over the possibility of recovering the lost goods. Beauty's sisters asked their father to bring back costly gifts, dresses and jewels; Beauty, however, having a premonition that things might not go as well as they hoped, asked only for a rose.

The recovery of the ship did turn out to be a disappointment. What little there was left was confiscated by creditors. Beauty's father turned back empty-handed, and on the way home became lost in the forest. Finally he saw a light in the distance and, following it, came upon a magnificent castle. The door was open and so he entered, finding there a tempting supper laid out before the fire. Giving in to his hunger, he ate it, and afterwards found his way to a bedroom. When he awoke next morning he discovered a fresh suit of clothes laid out for him along with breakfast. Marvelling at the generosity, for as yet he had met no one, he helped himself. Afterwards he went for a walk in the rose garden, and there remembered Beauty's request. Thinking to himself that at least one child's request need not go unanswered, he plucked a single, lovely rose for Beauty's sake.

At that very moment he heard a terrifying sound and turning saw a dreadful monster coming upon him. "How dare you steal my rose," cried Beast. "Is this the way to repay my kindness towards you?" The merchant fell to his knees trembling. He told the story of his misfortunes and how he had hoped to bring back at least one small thing for one of his children. Even in his terror the merchant wondered why, after so much generosity, Beast would quibble over a rose. Did Beauty ask for a small thing or a great thing? By comparison with fine clothes and jewels a rose is cheap, often free. It is just a trifle, if one of surpassing loveliness. But what of the *rosa mystica?* What is it? And what is its worth? What was Beauty really asking for? Did her father have the ability to grant her wish? And if he could not, who could?

Beast announced that the merchant's life was forfeit for attempting to steal the rose. Pleading for his children who would be orphaned, the merchant begged to be spared. Beast relented and agreed to pardon the merchant only if he would bring back Beauty in his stead. The merchant could not agree to such a bargain, but obtained permission to say goodbye to his family before meeting his death. Beast sent him home with a chest full of gold.

Beauty insisted that she herself should go—it was she after all who had asked for the rose—comforting her father by reminding him of Beast's generosity. Surely he meant them no harm. When she and her father arrived at the castle they found a sumptuous meal prepared for them. Again Beauty remarked on the kindness of the master. Then Beast entered from the garden. Beauty's soul shrank in dread at the sight of him, though she noticed that his eyes were so very sad.

What kind of a beast is Beast? If Beast is really Eros, as it would appear from the drawing power he exercised over the merchant, drawing him out of his way in the forest, towards the light, to the meal, to healing repose, to the garden, to the rose, it would be fitting that he should be either a bear (URsa) or a snake (URaeus, the sacred serpent of Egypt, from *uro,* asp; cf. Greek *oura,* indicating a tail, as in Ouroboros, the serpent biting its own tail). The bear is the most dangerous and "awe-ful" animal of the northern world, and as *Ursa major* (Big Dipper) and *Ursa minor* (Little Dipper) points to the center of the heavens (URanus, the God of heaven), the north or pole star. But the cumulative evidence of the various versions of the tale points to the ancient serpent (or dragon, also known as "the WORm") as the most likely candidate. Of all animals the snake has the richest and most varied symbolism, and is frequently designated simply as the Beast, as in the Great Beast of the Apocalypse. Beauty must have loved her father deeply to have answered "yes" when an enormous snake entered the room and asked if she would remain with him.

With that "yes" Beast declared her mistress of his castle, putting everything and everyone, himself included, at her bidding. Her father departed laden with three chests of gold and jewels and Beauty began to explore her new domain. Each evening Beast joined her for supper, and because of his unfailing kindness her fear slowly diminished, then went away. Each evening before he left her, he would ask her to marry him. "I cannot do so, Beast," she would reply. "You are good to me, but I am not in love with you." From the beginning Beast had asked her to be frank with him.

Beauty loved the nights best of all when she would invariably dream that a handsome young prince, who seemed strangely familiar, would come to her in the garden. Once an old woman came to her instead, telling her to look for beauty in the depths.

One morning she found a small oval mirror and, looking into it, saw her father lying ill. That night at supper she told Beast what she saw. Beast replied that when the pure of heart look into a mirror, they see what is. Beauty wanted to go to him and Beast, having promised to do her bidding, could not refuse. Only he begged her to return, for without her he would not live.

Her father improved rapidly after her arrival, but her wicked sisters, who had made bad marriages and were envious of Beauty's wealth, connived to make her prolong her stay, playing on her sympathy for her father. The weeks became months until one night Beauty had another dream. Again she was in the rose garden, but this time instead of the prince it was Beast she saw, lying on the ground wasted, near death. Beauty came to herself, realizing how much she cared for Beast. She rushed back to the castle and found him just as she had seen him in the dream, lying on the ground looking quite dead. She gathered him in her arms, begging him to recover and promising to be his wife. Then in desperation she went a few steps to the river for water, hoping to revive him. When she came back, there stood her prince.

Moral

There are many ways of reading the great tales; many lessons can be drawn from them. A question with which I have approached the story is: how can a woman find her own true mind? The tale tells me that the finding, the losing, and the finding again of her mind is bound up with her relationship to Eros. In one sense it seems that Eros as her mind is her very self, the dynamism at work within her (the root *er- means "to move or set in motion"), so that to find her mind is to come into her own. In another sense, since her mind can be found and lost and found again, Eros is a true other, but another without whom she cannot fully be (*er- is the root of 'are'). It matters then how she relates to what is her own. In that 'how' is revealed the mode and mood of her mind.

Her ORiginal or primORdial mind moves in ways most clearly suggested by metaphors of touch and hearing, rather than by sight. In that mode which is most properly her own, Eros simply gives himself to her. It is an effortless mode of knowing. It is bringing to mind what she has always known, a kind of knowing which is hardly distinguishable from being, but which requires, beyond effort, that she be "in touch," particularly with her own body as receptor/transmitter *par excellence.* Touch and hearing go hand in hand as modes of intimacy, while sight requires a certain distance and detachment in order to achieve perspective. By contrast, touch and hearing fail to achieve a point of view, but do have an awareness or feel for things which is more inclusive. What they know is unfocused yet subtle, diffuse yet pervasive, multiple yet familiar. It is the kind of knowing of which the Bible speaks when it says that "Adam knew Eve his wife" (Gn. 4:1) and when Mary objects to the angel, "How shall this be, seeing I know not a man?" (Lk. 1:34). Human intercourse includes both sexual intimacy (touching) and an intimacy of communication (hearing). In future it may well be by way of her original mind that we shall come to a better understanding of the mystery of the Word made flesh.

The potency of touch as a mode of knowing can be seen from the miracle of Jesus in which he cures a woman afflicted with hemorrhage (Lk. 8:41–48). The woman says to herself, "If I can but touch the fringe of his garment. . . ." And he says, stopping on his way to the house of Jairus, "Who touched me?" Peter objects, "Master, people are thronging you on every side," but Jesus interrupts: "No, someone touched me for I felt power go out of me." The woman, who was something of an "untouchable" because of the issue of blood, comes forward and confesses what she has done. Jesus replies: "Your faith has saved you." The whole incident plays on the significance or insignificance of touch. The crowd is pressing on Jesus but that sort of touch is insignificant; it is unknowing. The woman knows, even before the cure takes place— and it is said that she had tried many other cures over a period of twelve years to no avail—that one touch is all she needs. Why a touch? Why not a word, or even just a glance from Jesus? Is it because she is an untouchable that only a touch can heal? Is touch peculiarly related to the transmission of power? When Adam knew his wife, she conceived. There is a language of touch which has its own efficacy and which cannot be replaced by other forms of language.

In Chapter 10 of St. John's Gospel, Jesus likens his own to sheep who hear and recognize the voice of their shepherd. They know his voice because he calls them by name. They will not follow a stranger because they do not recognize the stranger's voice. And though the text does not say so explicitly, it may be surmised that the stranger is not able to call them by name. The stranger cannot speak to and call forth the very essence of the sheep. Psyche knew the voice of her beloved; he called her by name. And yet she fell prey to the voices of her sisters. Or did she? Would she have listened to them if they had not reminded her of the ORacle, which was also the voice of her beloved? Was her plight not akin to that of Eve, where the divine voice itself invites her in opposite directions? Or, putting it another way, did her own experience of her lover tell her one thing, while her culture (all the negative fantasies about snakes and dragons) insisted on the opposite? But what could explain her betrayal of her own experience if not a confusion which has its ultimate root, at least apparently, in a conflict located within the divine reality, and which finds its occasion in the limitations inherent to her particular mode of knowing, her inability to see.

Faith comes through hearing (Rm. 10:17), not through seeing. Faith belongs to the modes of intimacy, not to the critical mode of detachment and distance. It is what Kierkegaard would call subjective truth, the truth of the subject or self.[7] It is truth between subjects or selves. It is different from the kinds of truth which pertain between subject and object or between object and object. When Semele and

Psyche forsake the modes of intimacy and insist upon seeing, they turn the beloved into an object and the relationship becomes one of subject to object: from I—Thou to I—It.[8] But no amount of scrutiny of an 'It' will ever yield a 'Thou.' What happens to Soul when she loses her Thou?

The temptation to look at the forbidden is in all ways like unto the temptation to take and eat of the forbidden Tree. Was it not inevitable that Semele and Psyche, like Eve their mother, should succumb? Were we given eyes that we should not see? If touch and hearing are in a certain paradoxical sense effortless modes of knowing,[9] seeing is the mode of effort. The known (now unknown) is not given to sight, but is mediated through an image: a lightning bolt, a God of heartbreaking beauty, an empty box, a Beast. It is required that she lEARn to see beyond (and through) what is seen. She cannot fully awake from the deathlike sleep into which she has fallen until the eye of the heart (Eph. 1:18) opens.

The way of seeing is in the first instance (Semele) a tragic mistake. The human instrument is too fragile to withstand the divine vision. Why is it so? Does sight reveal something which touch and hearing had mercifully cloaked? Yet is it not strange that the immediacy of God should be bearable, while the image is unbearable? Life as it comes to us day by day and moment by moment is measured to our size. But to seize the whole of it in a vision: would it be too terrible to endure? Would we be overwhelmed by grief and longing for what might have been? Would it appear pointless and empty? Or would we confront Beast?

The way of seeing is in the second instance (Beauty) a path of redemption. Once Psyche has forsaken her original mind for the certainty and control which sight promises (an empty promise?), the only way back to her own true mind is through the suffering of vision and the vision of suffering. What does it mean to look at Beast? What does it mean to come to love Beast? What does it mean to wed Beast?

Whereas touch and hearing brought her joy, vision brings suffering. Semele is blinded and burned by her vision; Psyche is rapt but griefstricken, despairing, finally rendered unconscious by hers; Beauty is frightened and repelled, but not so much that she fails to notice what shines beneath the surface. The suffering of vision has both an objective and a subjective component. It is too much and too little: it is everything at once, but only an image of everything; it is a grasp of the whole, but one involving loss of the gift.

A tragic mistake can however become a path of redemption. The suffering of vision can become a vision of suffering. What does it mean to look at Beast? The tale is most discreet so far as a description of Beast is concerned. Perhaps the look of Beast cannot be captured by words. What we are given is a series of reactions on the part of the merchant, then on the part of Beauty. What we are given is not the look of Beast, which we must find out for ourselves, but an indication of how one may look at Beast. From the beginning Beauty notices the difference between the terrifying outward appearance and the generosity, kindness, and respectfulness of the actions. She is not afraid to remain with Beast, but she cannot bring herself to become intimate with him. When she consents to remain with him, he makes himself her servant where he might have established himself as master. This too is not lost on her, though not yet really understood. The wisdom which comes to her in dreams, the fair prince and the words of the wise old woman, reveals an awareness which is still unconscious, which has not yet become a "seeing." When her heart calls her away from him, he allows her to go but reminds her that he will not live without her. She does not truly hear him; her touch and hearing have been numbed. Swayed by her sisters, she is still able to forget. Another dream comes to her. This time Beast appears in the place of the handsome prince. The look of Beast, the suffering of vision has been allowed to penetrate the inmost soul, the level of the unconscious. That coalescence of Beast and the prince in the unconscious is the lightning bolt which opens the eye of the heart. She sees Beast for the first time as he really is, and she sees the plight he is in and for which she is responsible. It is this moment of vision which matters, the transformation of Beast into prince being but the outward confirmation. It is a saving vision. It frees the prince from his beastly condition; it awakens Psyche from her long sleep.

Endnotes

1. C. G. Jung, 1929. Commentary on "The Secret of the Golden Flower." In *Collected Works,* 13:60.
2. C. G. Jung, 1927. Mind and Earth. In *Collected Works,* 10:81.
3. A close study of Plato reveals a structural pattern to the dialogues corresponding to Plato's theory of levels of knowledge: (1) *doxa,* common opinions; (2) *techne,* how to; (3) *episteme,* what; (4) *dianoia,* why or why not. After a negative result at the fourth level of inquiry, it is characteristic for Plato to introduce a myth and to cap it by pointing to Socrates. The implication seems to be that beyond what can be argued rationally, there is what can only be shown imaginally and existentially.
4. Walter F. Otto. 1933. *Dionysus: Myth and Cult* (Dallas: Spring Publications, 1981), pp. 69–72.
5. Cf. Jung's *Collected Works* 7:332, 338; 10:81, 698; 16:538n.
6. Robert Graves translates: "Nor hope a son-in-law of mortal birth/But a dire mischief, viperous and fierce. . . ." *Greek Myths* (Baltimore: Penguin, 1955).
7. In *Concluding Unscientific Postscript,* Part II, ch. 2 ("The Subjective Truth, Inwardness; Truth is Subjectivity") and in *Sickness unto Death,* Pt. I.
8. Cf. Martin Buber's *I and Thou,* Pt. I.
9. Touch and hearing are effortless in a paradoxical sense because despite the immediacy and givenness of the known, they require the utmost development and refinement of the human knower, precisely in what constitutes her "humanity" (cf. jên (1), humanheartedness). Note how the human being (2) reaches out from above and from below (3). Ezra Pound translates jên as "humanheartedness" in his *Confucius* (New Directions).

1. 仁
2. 亻
3. 仁

Chapter Three

No, That Is Not It

The woman with the hole in her chest moves into the arms of her lover and is healed instantly. She draws back from the embrace and asks of a third person, not her lover: "Is this it?" A voice answers: "No, that is not it."

How could it not be it? Is she not healed from her great wound? Perplexed, as though she has heard it wrong, she repeats the scene. Once again she has the gaping hole in her chest. Once again she moves into the arms of her lover. Once again she is healed. She draws back and repeats her question: "Is this it?" Once again the voice answers: "No, that is not it."

Unable to comprehend the "no," she repeats the scene a third time: the wound, the embrace, the healing, the question, the response. There is a kind of finality to the third time. This time she must accept the response even if it continues to baffle her. She reflects on her question and realizes that she deserves to be baffled. What did she mean by "it"? "Is this *what*?" Is the "it" of the question the same as the "it" of the response? Is "it" her soul?

She knows that the "this" of the question refers to the healing embrace, and she is baffled by the "not that" of the response. It cannot be an absolute "no" for the healing does occur and is confirmed through repetition. The healing embrace must be at least part of "it." Is there something else, something missing, something left behind? She thinks back to the three versions of the story and asks herself what may have been left behind. The answer leaps out at her: all that female rage. The outraged goddesses, the enraged sisters, what is it all about? Has something of herself, of her own soul, been denied and forgotten as she ascends into the heaven of Eros?

51

Only in the Greek version do the sisters have names and stories of their own. By the time of Apuleius' tale of Psyche and Eros, and the much later French version of Beauty and the Beast, the sisters have been left so far behind that they have degenerated to stereotypes of wicked anger and jealousy. We are glad to see them defeated and dismissed as we rejoice in Psyche's heavenly nuptials. But now a voice reminds us that after all life is not so simple as all that. We are not so simple as all that. What we have left behind or, in psychological terms, repressed, has a way of returning when the time is ripe.

Two of the sisters, Agave and Autonoë, have parallel stories. Both are taken with the maenadic frenzy; both lose their sons in remarkably similar ways. Autonoë's son, Actaeon, dared to look upon the naked Artemis while she bathed in a forest spring. Artemis turned him into a stag and his own pack of hounds tore him apart. Pentheus, Agave's son, succeeded Cadmus as ruler of Thebes. Disgusted by the effeminacy of Dionysos and by the wild abandon of the maenads, mortified that his mother and his aunts had joined them, yet curious as to the nature of their orgy, he dared to eavesdrop on their revels. The maenads fell upon him. Each of his aunts tore off an arm at the shoulder; his own mother wrenched off his head and, thinking it to be a lion's head, displayed the trophy with pride until the divine madness left her and human grief (the name Pentheus comes from *penthos,* grief) took its place.

Actaeon's misdeed seems almost innocent by comparison to that of Pentheus. Whereas Pentheus set out with the intention to spy and to mock, Actaeon was almost a victim of circumstances. He happened upon the naked Artemis bathing in a sylvan spring. But, unlike the reverent Anchises, who averted his eyes from the beauty of Aphrodite, knowing the sight would unman him, Actaeon dared to look at the forbidden. What does it mean to look upon the nakedness of Artemis? Artemis is pure nature, remote, beyond human reach. If her name is AR + Themis, she is the original, creative order of things; she is how things are. To look upon her nakedness would be to look into the very essence of reality, but in its uncivilized, inhuman, raw state. Can that sight be borne? She is that part of Inanna which corresponds to the unhewn, green Tree. She is Mistress of the Wild Things and, like Lilith, presides over childbirth and death, and all threshold experiences. Actaeon, whose name means "shore dweller" and who is himself a hunter, would be especially drawn to her. But to turn towards her, particularly for one who has never quite gotten past the threshold of consciousness, and to look unabashedly, is to be drawn into the greater

Reality. He can no longer unlock his gaze. He reverts to her world; he goes back to the wild. To touch or even to look upon the sacred is to become sacred. He turns into a stag, an animal especially sacred to Artemis, and one highly revered in shamanic cultures as a means of magical transport between heaven and earth. In one sense he is exalted by being drawn into the divine reality, but in another sense he loses his hold on human consciousness and slips back to a lower, animal form. He also reverts from hunter to hunted, torn apart by his own hounds. The rending and devouring seem to indicate that there is no end to the reversion. The tenuous human identity disintegrates before our very eyes.

Pentheus meets essentially the same fate though his death is rendered even more horrible because he is torn apart while still retaining human shape (though it is questionable whether or not the maenads who fall upon him recognize him as human), and more particularly because the instruments of his destruction are his female kin, led by his own mother. The greater horror of his death corresponds qualitatively to the greater sin. Disgust and scorn, accompanied by prurient curiosity, testify to an irreligiousness more pronounced than that of Actaeon.

But suppose we look at these dreadful events from the point of view of the mothers, not so much of the human mothers who have destroyed their sons as of the female principle destroying her own effort at soul-making. Why she performs the heinous deed is clear if we think of the culpability of Actaeon and Pentheus. Both were violators of the female essence. Euripides has it that Actaeon boasted of being a greater hunter than Artemis (*Bacchae* 340). In terms of mind it amounts to a claim that rational inquiry surpasses intuition in its pursuit of truth. Intuition is often symbolized by the dog with its nose close to the ground, and the maenads are likened to hounds (*Bacchae* 731). Myth hints that a rational cast of mind which spurns its intuitional matrix is destroyed by those very intuitions it thinks to outdistance. Does it also mean that rational thinking is improper or impossible for a woman? Only if it sets her at odds with that deeper mind which is called Dionysos. The sins of the sons are the outcome of the sins of the mothers who had slandered Semele and Dionysos by denying his divine origin. It is equivalent to Eve's denial of the serpent.

To speak this way of "the sins of the mothers" seems a terrible accusation if we consider that the name Autonoë, meaning "thinking for herself" or "with a mind of her own," represents an ideal for modern woman. *Autos* as "self" or "self-same" stems from the idea of being self-propelled, acting or being directed from within. *Nous* comes from the root *gno-*, meaning "to know." In the development of Greek philosophy, *nous* comes to mean the highest form of mind.[1] It is an immediate intuitive grasp of the very essence of things or it is what lies behind our ability to make correct judgments, even when or especially when we cannot explain how we know. It is the foundation of all other forms of knowing in that it is the knowledge of the givens (the axioms, the first principles, the presuppositions) from which discursive reasoning begins; the intuitive grasp of the whole which enables us to gestalt perceptions; the imaginative leap which preshapes and motivates technical knowledge; the awareness which guides the ethical pursuit of the good; the recognition of a call at the heart of being. It is also the goal of all other forms of knowing, being the closest possible relationship between knower and known which can still be distinguished as mind. In other words it is a vision of unity, or it may be that the final desire of the mind is what from our side of the divide between reality and unreality looks to be extinction, unity itself.

So what is wrong with "thinking for herself" or "a mind of her own"? Actaeon's story is our clue. What is wrong with his looking at the nakedness of Artemis? Is it not a storied example of the immediate intuitive grasp of the very essence of things? How does a woman feel the wrongness of this occurrence? She resents a taking of what has not been given. In terms of mind it may well mean that the knowledge of simple essences or wholes, while legitimately desired by the mind, may not be within human reach or "grasp." It may also mean that essential knowledge is transformative knowledge and that the "shore-dweller," poised between dry land and sea, between conscious and unconscious, is in an especially precarious position. What is not there for the taking may yet be received by those to whom it is given, however. And it may be that the nature of the transformation, whether it should be called creative or destructive, depends very much upon the manner in which it is suffered. Had Actaeon respected the nakedness of the Goddess, not wishing to take advantage uninvited of a moment of defenselessness, would not that very movement have prepared him for the gift? If we think of Actaeon as the expression of Autonoë's mind, what is wrong is her lack of self-respect, for, psychologically speaking, the simple essence or whole which the mind seeks is the Self.

The name Agave may be a combination of *agh-*, the root of 'awe', an emotion which mingles wonder and reverence with dread or fear, and *aiw-*, the root meaning "vital force, life, or eternity." "Awe before the vital force," which is at once the force of creation and of destruction, would make sense as an interpretation of her name if we think of the story of Pentheus. It must certainly have been the effect produced by Euripides' *Bacchae* on his Greek audience. Insofar as Pentheus is the projection of Agave's mind, however, we would have to conclude that awe before the vital force is precisely what he lacked and is the reason for his destruction. From that perspective Agave would be guilty not just of a lack of self-respect as was her sister, Autonoë, but of self-hatred. Pentheus despises the female essence, all the while being drawn into its power by a prurient curiosity. Agave's reaction against herself could be likened to Inanna's grieving over the Tree which she begs Gilgamesh to chop down and to Eve's shame over her relationship to the serpent.

Agave in the person of Pentheus hates what she is. Why? Perhaps the ambivalence of awe provides a clue. The vital force inspires not only wonder and reverence but dread and fear. How can we hold such opposite emotions in combination? Actually, experience teaches that the opposites commingle naturally. It requires no effort at all. Almost any strong feeling will upon analysis reveal two faces. That which we love we also hate; what we need is what we flee. What is difficult is to look steadily at both faces. Usually, when one face shows itself, the other face hides. We are conscious of the one, while the other sinks into but continues to work in the unconscious. As Pentheus, Agave consciously despises the female essence, while unconsciously (as Agave) exacting a terrible revenge upon the desecrator. Instinctively, she destroys a mind so inimical to her deepest self, then is griefstricken over her loss of mind. What would restore her mind would be a cultivation of awe, a conscious holding together of the opposites. If Eve could put together God and the serpent, if Inanna could join the green tree to the hewn tree, if Agave could realize that what destroys is what creates, that what creates is what destroys, she could perhaps find solace for her grief. More than that, she might even find joy in her grief!

The sin of the sisters and the tragedy of the sons turns upon the rejection of Dionysos. Even in the case of Actaeon, while it is Artemis who turns him into a stag, it is Dionysos who works through the fifty hounds to dismember him. Dionysos is the God of Nysa. Nysa has been variously located in Arabia, Egypt, Ethiopia, Euboea, India, Lydia, Syria, Thrace, on Mt. Parnassus, on Mt. Helicon, and in the Land of the Sun. Walter F. Otto was convinced that the name refers to a female fairyland, "a divine mountain country in a distant land of fantasy, similar to the land of the Hyperboreans."[2] The women who inhabit that land are Nysai, the nurses of Dionysos. We have already related the 'n' to the fish and the snake, to the act of swallowing, and to the nasalized sound which conduces to trance. What about the 's' which also resembles the snake in both form and sound?

Hugh Moran relates the Hebrew *sin* 𐤔 or *shin* 𐤔 not to "tooth," the usual translation, but to *seh* (Assyrian *su'u*), a truncated singular form for the Hebrew collective noun, *tson*, "a flock of sheep or goats." Related derivatives are *sim* (unlucky, inauspicious), *senah* (hatred, aversion), *sa-ar* (hairy), *sa'ir* (he-goat, satyr, goat-man), *shin* (urine), and *Se'ir* (Edom, "the goat land"). There are in Hebrew various roots in *sig* and *shik* (cf. the Greek name for the letter 's', *sigma*), meaning "to become drunk, to go astray, to be mad, insane, looney." In Sumerian *sig* is a he-goat, while *Sin* is the Moon God.[3] We have then in Nysa (NS) a combination of goat and fish or water-snake, the sign of Capricorn, ♑. The odd figure of the Goat-Fish unites the heights and the depths, for the goat scales mountain heights, associated in the ancient mind with heaven and spirit, while the snake and the fish belong to the watery depths of the unconcious. There is also a paradoxical union of light and darkness coincident with the winter solstice which ushers in the time of Capricorn, when the Light re-emerges triumphantly out of deepest darkness. How thought-provoking it is that the birth of Christ should be symbolically situated in the time of Capricorn just after the winter solstice.[4] The two sisters who recognize the divinity of Dionysos, his mother, Semele, and his foster-mother, Ino, are the terms of that vertical axis extending from the mountain heaven to the watery depths. Dionysos himself brings his mother up from Hades to the Olympian heaven where, immortalized, she receives the title, Semele Thyone, which means something like "earth ecstasy."[5] Ino ends her earthly existence by plunging into the sea to save her son, Melicertes, whose name means "sweet power" or "power of sweetness" (= mead = Dionysos). There she receives the title Leucothea, the White Goddess. Agave and Autonoë, who deny the divinity of Dionysos, are nevertheless bound to him, possessed by him, in a way that is destructive not of their mortal lives but of their very souls.

It seems that the power of Dionysos is irresistible, as witnessed by the daughters of Minyas who attempted to refuse an invitation to the revels, preferring to remain sedately faithful to their husbands' rule. While sitting at their looms they began to hear the music of flutes, drums, and cymbals. All at once ivy and grape leaves wove themselves onto the looms and the ceiling dripped honey and milk. The madness seized them and, casting lots for which of their sons should be victim, they fastened upon Hippasus, Leucippe's little son, tearing him apart

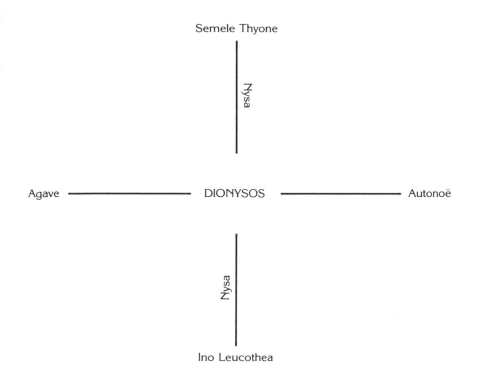

and devouring him. The destructive and cannibalistic frenzy is not confined to those who scorn Dionysos, however. It appears to be an integral part of the mystery, belonging to the essence, since it was the fate of Dionysos himself to be torn apart at birth by the Titans at the instigation of Hera and to be reconstituted and brought back to life by his grandmother, Rhea. It is typical maenadic behavior both to nurture and to destroy, to suckle wild beasts at their breasts and to tear them to pieces with their bare hands, eating them raw. They exhibit the rawness of life and death, nature in the raw. By including their own sons in the wild melee, what they show forth is the profound circularity of life and death. What brings into life is what destroys; life and death are one and the same. If the Goddess is Life, she is also Death, and Life again.

What is the Dionysiac madness? In Greek it is called *mainomenos*. It is a form of mind, but one which is not human, and one which is in some profound sense angry toward human being, as shown by the two basic meanings of our own word 'mad'. The root of 'mad' is *mei-*, which means "to change, go, or move," as in permeate, permute, transmute, molt, mutate, migrate. *Mei- is also the root of 'mew', and it is under the form of a sea mew, a type of gull, that Ino saves Odysseus from drowning. The Dionysiac mind is one which moves past human boundaries, and it is perhaps the dissolution of those boundaries, of the properly human form, which feels to us like anger if we identify with the human form, or like ecstasy if we identify with the mind which moves past it. It ranges both above and below the human limits into the unthinkable and the unconditional, the unbearable and the inexhaustible, the immoral and the immortal, the outrageous and the outstanding.

In its positive aspects the Dionysiac mind is ecstasy and intoxication which lift us out of our cares and ordinary limitations. It frees us of our burdens and duties. With that mind the maenads skim the mountain tops, dancing to an irresistible music. It is a plunge into the freedom and energy of God. It is also true mentation, the inspired genius which comes from tapping the very source of creativity. There is a Boeotian legend to the effect that when Dionysos cannot be found, he is with the Muses. He is indeed the mind of the Muses (soothsaying, poetry, the arts) or the musical mind which, as indicated by the root *mu- ("that which cannot be seen or spoken"), is mind beyond the range of the human, that is, mind beyond the range of control, explanation, or comprehension, though not beyond apprehension and exploration; in other words, irrational or superrational mind. It is the deeper and larger mind which gives birth to, sustains and supports, and finally tears apart, chews up, and swallows into semi-oblivion a rational thought process (a philosophy, a scientific theory, a political system, a psychology), only to spit forth another fresher one in its stead.

Both men and women participate in the Dionysiac mind, though myth insists that it belongs to women or women belong to it in a special way. Men too can be possessed by it, as was Ino's husband, Athamas, who under the spell of the madness slew his own son, Learchus, mistaking him for a white stag. Transfixing him with an arrow, Athamas tore his still quivering body limb from limb. It was this murderous act which precipitated Ino's plunge into the sea to save her second son, Melicertes. Then there is the story of Lycurgus whom Rhea struck with the madness for having resisted Dionysos and his retinue. Lycurgus axed down his own son, Dryas, mistaking him for a vine, which he proceeded to prune, lopping off nose, ears, fingers, and toes. If we look at the names of the sons, we see that Dryas is indeed a tree which is at its root a truth, Learchus is indeed a white ruler which is at its root a light.[6] Why must the tree be pruned? So that it may grow stronger and bear more fruit. Why must the white light be broken up? So that we may see the colors.

The male figures which belong properly to the mystery of Dionysos are satyrs and sileni, not the hero types. These are nature spirits, often depicted as half human and half goat or horse. They are ithyphallic, with pointed ears and flowing tails, and sometimes represented with the legs of a horse or goat (the Christian devil). Through the fifth century B.C. 'satyrs' (goat-men) and 'sileni' (moon-men) were used interchangeably. Later they were differentiated, the sileni appearing as ugly, coarse-featured, bald old men, while the satyrs were young, goat-legged, and focussed on their huge erections. Both are given to wine, music, and lusting after maenads. These are men who are at the service of the Goddess, both in the sense of servicing her as studs and glorying in the delights of nature, and in the higher sense of dedicating themselves to the female principle, the feminine mind. It is with a sure instinct that in Plato's *Symposium* (215a and sq.), the drunken Alcibiades compares Socrates to Marsyas the satyr, who bewitches mankind with his music, and to Silenos, the tutor of Dionysos, not only in terms of his looks but in terms of what lies within. It seems to have been common practice among Greek craftsmen to make, with more than a touch of Socratic irony, droll little statues of sileni which open down the middle, revealing beautiful images of gods contained within.

The whole structure of the *Symposium* centers on Socrates as a Silenos figure, illuminating simultaneously both the inner meaning of Socrates and of Silenos. The setting of the *Symposium* is a dinner party to celebrate the prize Agathon has won with his first tragedy. After dinner the guests decide against trying to outdrink one another, still suffering as they are from the excesses of the previous night and readily acknowledging Socrates to be the champion in that respect, and also dispense with the usual flute music, preferring in its stead to entertain one another by making speeches in praise of Eros. Implied by the substitution is a symbolic equivalence between intoxication and music and the praise of Eros. The worship of Eros also comes through as the secret purpose of wine, women, and song. Each guest makes his speech culminating with that of Socrates, who on the one hand claims that love is the one thing he understands (177d), but when his turn comes simply recounts what he has learned from a woman named Diotima (201d).

It is doubly striking that Socrates, whose only claim to wisdom was consciousness of his ignorance (*Apology* 21d), should pretend to understand Eros, and that the same Socrates, master of irony and of the art of self-examination, should then proffer an understanding which he had got second-hand, from a woman. What does it tell us? Perhaps two things. First, that an understanding of Eros is not like ordinary understanding since it is compatible with a consciousness of ignorance; second, that there is a feminine form of wisdom which goes beyond what can be achieved through rational dialectic.[7] What Socrates has received from Diotima is both not his own in that he did not/could not figure it out for himself, and most profoundly his own since it emerges autonomously from his innermost, feminine soul.

Socrates has no sooner finished his speech and received the crown than Alcibiades bursts into the room drunk and proceeds to make a further speech not in praise of Eros, but of Socrates. Whereas he began by bragging that Socrates was in love with him (Socrates as satyr), he ends by confessing that it is he who has been chasing after Socrates. Socrates pretends to be the lover but is in fact the beloved. A paradoxical identification is made between the ugly Silenos figure and the beautiful God. Once again Capricorn appears, uniting heights and depths.

Satyrs and sileni are at home with the mystery of Dionysos while the male hero, such as Perseus, Theseus, or their older counterpart, Gilgamesh, must protest against it. The prehuman and the superhuman are nurtured by the mystery, but the middle range, which we call the properly human and which is exemplified by heroic achievement, is threatened by it. Insofar as Hera inspires the heroic, as her name suggests, and represents that part of the female essence which wants the male to break away from her and to become something in his own right,[8] we can understand better the deep-seated enmity of Hera for Dionysos and for all those who are related to him in any way. A son must separate himself from his mother and sisters in order to become a man, to achieve his male identity; virtue must extricate itself from instinct; the rational mind must achieve distance and detachment to arrive at lucidity. Dionysos, however, belongs to the women, and the women belong to him. He is woman's inner masculinity; he is female mind, or the mind that operates unconsciously, instinctively, which insofar as it can be made conscious is also Eros.

Perseus' express reason for setting out to cut off the Gorgon Medusa's head was in order to protect his mother, Danaë, from a bad marriage with Polydectes. So it would seem that severance from the mother was not uppermost in his mind. But on closer inspection it was he who made the proposal, not Polydectes, who had asked for horses

as a gift towards a proposed marriage to another woman, Hippodameia.
If Perseus is in no position to make a gift of a horse, how can he hope
to travel to he knows not where to slay the Gorgon? He has no money,
no horse, no energy. He is living with his mother in some kind of servile
dependency. It is doubtless that very situation of dependency which
conjures up in him the face of the Devourer. Having made his boast,
he finds a powerful friend in Athena, the sworn enemy of Medusa. She
gives him her bright shield, warning him never to look at the Gorgon
directly, for whoever looks at her directly is turned to stone, but to look
only at her reflection in the shield. Hermes gives him a sickle with which
to cut off the head, but he still needs winged sandals, a magic wallet
in which to carry the head, and Hades' cap of invisibility to be able to
make the journey safely. These he must obtain from the Stygian nymphs,
and only the Graeae, a triad of old women who are the Gorgons' sisters,
know the whereabouts of the nymphs. Sneaking up upon the Graeae,
he snatches the single tooth and eye they share among themselves
and refuses to give them up until the Graeae show him the way.

Having obtained the sandals, wallet, and cap from the nymphs,
he journeys on to the land of the Hyperboreans where he completes
his task successfully by following Athena's instructions. On the way
home he finds his future wife, Andromeda, chained to a sea-cliff, offered
there as a propitiation to a female sea-monster, angered because Andromeda's mother, Cassiopeia, has boasted that she and her daughter
were more beautiful than the Nereids. Perseus repeats the slaying of
the Gorgon by beheading the sea-monster, who has been deceived by
his shadow on the sea.

Whether consciously or unconsciously, by his boast Perseus
exhibits the cunning of a Medusa, extricating himself from his mother's
arms in such a way as to retain her favor. He convinces her that it is
for her sake, to save her from the evil Polydectes, that he must go on
a conveniently long and distant journey. Thus he ensures his manhood
and frees himself sufficiently to find his own soul in the person of the
fair Andromeda, whose name, interestingly enough, echoes that of
Medusa as "ruler of men." Does the repetition mean that the liberation
was a deception? Yes and no. He does set out on the adventure of life.
He goes his own way. He performs the heroic deed, slaying the monster
from whose body sprang Chrysaor, the hero of the golden sword, and
Pegasus, the winged horse. In the one decisive act he both achieves
his identity (Perseus = "destroyer") and frees up his spiritual energy.
He returns home safely, finding and winning his bride along the way

of the return. And yet the name Andromeda hints that he finds and weds what he had thought to conquer. It seems that the cunning Medusa has ruled the entire drama from beginning to end.

Of the three Gorgon sisters, Stheno the Mighty and Euryale the Far-leaping are immortal, while Medusa the cunning Queen is their mortal part.[9] Only through Medusa can they be defeated and then only temporarily, as the story of Perseus suggests. They are depicted with huge round faces, serpents for hair as well as serpents entwined about the waist, boar's tusks for teeth, a hideous wide grin with lolling tongue, and great goggling eyes. To meet the gaze of a Gorgon is to be petrified by fear; at least such is the conviction of the Greeks. In India the *kirttimukha* or "Face of Glory," in China the *t'ao-t'ieh* or "Glutton," and in Mesoamerica the jaguar-sarcophagus or "flesh eater", are objects of contemplation and protection for the wise. In the legend of the Face of Glory, Shiva promises that no one who fails to worship the Face will over obtain his grace.[10] Kali ("Time") in her terrible aspect is another analog of the Gorgon figure and, strange as it may seem to our sensibilities, has her worshippers who find in her a wonder beyond good and evil and an ineffable peace.

According to myth the Gorgons are daughters of Phorcys, the Old Man of the Sea, and Ceto, the sea-monster from whom the whales get their name. The grandparents are Earth (Gaia) and Sea (Pontus). At bottom they are the elemental powers of earth and water from which all life flows and to which it returns. What they lack is air and fire. Despite the overwhelmingly negative connotations given to them by the Greeks, they are profoundly ambivalent figures. They are "gorgeous," amazingly beautiful on the one hand and a dizzying whirlpool, abyss, or giant maw on the other. They "grin," making a cheery face like their sisters, the Graces or Charites, and a rictus or grimace like their sisters, the Graeae or Grey Ones. They are overly toothed and toothless. To look into their eyes is to see too much and too little. The inhumanity of that "too much and too little" has a paralyzing effect, robbing a person of the ability to act, to do, to create, even as it confers a peace and a wisdom.

If, as I see it, the maenads are embodiments of the Gorgon reality in all its ambivalence, beautiful as they dance with the rhythm of Euryale, terrible as they tear their victims with the inhuman strength of Stheno, marvelous as they prophesy with the serpent-wisdom of Medusa, it is no wonder that they cannot take their own productions seriously. They are quick to destroy the offspring they have so tenderly nurtured. While the male tends to take his work very seriously, finding in it his identity as the OFFspring of the female and his mode of being severed and distanced from her, the female cannot sever herself from that which she is, which is life-and-death all rolled up in one. She may smile either in indulgence or in scornful pity at the male as he puffs himself up over the supposed importance of his words, deeds, and works. She knows how quickly they will disappear into insignificance. Her sorrow is that she cannot take her own words, deeds and works seriously enough to accomplish anything.

The sexual differentiation of the son from the mother creates in him an urgency to find out who *he* is, apart from her, and above and beyond the natural given with which she is symbolically identified. He experiences the devouring aspect of the Terrible Mother as a threat to both *what* and *who* he is (or wishes to be). The girl child, on the other hand, by her sexual identification with the mother and her symbolic identification with nature does not experience quite the same urgency or quite the same threat. She not only risks being devoured but participates in the reality of the devourer, so aptly represented in the East by the monster which devours itself until all that is left is a Face, and so possesses an innate understanding of the necessity of a rhythm between birthing and killing, the ontological give-and-take. A human girl child is not pure nature, however. As a human being she has within her the possibility of transcendence, and her fulfillment as a human being wants something more than a living out of natural rhythms. A boy child is not pure transcendence either. Something in him yearns for and can find the highest spiritual fulfillment in a submission to nature. If there can be a Lao Tzu or a Meister Eckhart, a male realization of the feminine principle, can there not be a female realization of the masculine principle as well?

Athena, the thoroughly patriarchal female, born from her father's head, as friend of heroes and a mighty heroine herself, both expresses a female realization of the masculine principle and, understandably, bears an implacable hatred for the Medusa, who is the nemesis of hero and heroine alike. Yet even Athena, for all her wisdom, skill and strategy, does not escape the cunning of Medusa, who may be interpreted psychologically as her shadow self, that part of her which is unacknowledged and unintegrated consciously, but is lived out unconsciously. When Perseus brings back the head of Medusa in his magic wallet, he gives it to Athena who affixes it to her breastplate, which, according to Robert Graves, is a goatskin bag containing a humanheaded serpent and protected by the Gorgon mask. Some say that she even wears the flayed skin of the Medusa as a cloak. The serpent-child, Erichthonius (ER of the earth), so reminiscent not only of the Gorgons but of Dionysos, who was born horned and crowned with serpents, is the closest Athena ever came to bearing a son. Story has it that Hephaestus embraced her and ejaculated against her thigh. In disgust she pushed him away and his semen fell to the earth which bore Erichthonius, and whom Athena agreed to adopt. Later, Athena fastened to his serpent body two phials of Medusa's blood, the blood from her left side having a curative power strong enough to raise the dead back to life, and the blood from the right side having the power to destroy. The Medusa thus comes more and more to the fore of the one who is "owl-eyed" and "Gorgon-faced," like a long shadow which walks ahead of her.

Yet Athena knows something which the Gorgon does not. She knows how to distinguish between image and reality. What she teaches Perseus is that if the distinction between image and reality can be clearly grasped, he can follow the image in such a way as to make safe contact with the reality. The depotentiated image gives guidance without casting a fatal spell. What the sea-monster does not realize, because she does not separate image and reality, is that to kill the image is not to kill the reality. "If you meet the Buddha on the road, kill him." The religious mind, which holds image and reality together in unity ("he that hath seen me hath seen the Father" [John 14:9]), is shocked at the proposal. The Medusa's gradual takeover of Athena after her so-called death, her reappearance in the form of the beautiful Andromeda, makes me wonder to what extent image and reality can indeed be separated (can Athena wear the Gorgon mask without becoming Gorgon-like?), to what extent the image loses its power when we realize that it is only an image. Is it not rather like the Hydra which, when one head is severed, sprouts forth two more in its place?

Theseus, carried off to Crete with a group of Greek youths to be sacrificed to the Minotaur, got King Minos to agree to revoke the tribute if he could defeat the Minotaur with his bare hands. What Theseus could not defeat by himself was the labyrinth at the center of which waited the Minotaur. Ariadne, daughter of Minos and Pasiphaë and half-sister to the Minotaur, fell in love with Theseus and promised to help him find his way through the labyrinth if he would take her back to Athens as his wife. For this she had a magic ball of thread which she tied to the entrance way. The ball of thread would roll along of its own accord, twisting and turning its way through the labyrinth, guiding

Theseus to the innermost sanctuary where he must face the Minotaur. Should he succeed he could find his way out again by rolling up the ball. When Theseus emerged triumphant Ariadne embraced him and, together with the remaining Greek youths, they fled to their ship and escaped. Some days later they stopped over at an island called Dia ("goddess"?), later renamed Naxos ("night"? cf. nix, noxious), where Theseus abandoned Ariadne who lay sleeping on the beach. No one knows for sure why he forsook her, whose name means "most pure" (from *ariagne*), though it may well be that Theseus was ashamed to bring back to Athens a priestess of what the Greeks considered to be a disgustingly primitive, dark, and female religion. Some say that Ariadne died there in the pangs of childbirth, others that she hanged herself, still others that Dionysos found her there and married her as his own true and only wife.

Ariadne functioned as a true soul-guide for Theseus. She showed him the way to the center of the earth through the labyrinth, which the Hopi Indians call the "Mother Earth" symbol, where he met its secret under the form of the man-bull, the animal nature of man, his life and his death all in one. The labyrinth is the shape of the mystery of the body and of embodied existence. It is the form of the brain, the heart, the ear, the kidney, the intestines; one might even say that it is the form of nature.[11] Ariadne's thread, the red thread of energy which runs through things, events, and lives, which she revealed to him, is the Tao. She gave him the precious secret of female religion. He used her to obtain his freedom from the thralldom of earth, then abandoned her. What happens to the man who uses his own soul? What happens to the man who forsakes his own soul? On his return to Greece he forgot to hoist the white sail, the agreed upon sign between himself and his father, Aegeus, that he returned safe and sound. Seeing the black sail coming into the harbor, Aegeus fainted in grief, falling head-long into the sea. It may be that the man who betrays his own soul, despising her earthiness, may find his own male religion, the mystery of father and son whose secret is spirit, disrupted.

But Ariadne is no innocent either. Did she not betray family and homeland in her love for Theseus? There is a real sense in which she deserves what she gets from Theseus. It is a justice of the earth; she reaps what she sows. It makes me wonder why Dionysos, who as Zagreus seems closely akin to the Minotaur, chooses her for his bride. Does he want to succumb to Theseus? Is it that her betrayal is essentially different from that of Agave and Autonoë? Or is there some special hidden sense to being chosen as the bride of Dionysos? Ariadne does not deny the divine character of her religion; she is its priestess. But she opens the secret of that religion to one whose only intention is to overthrow it. She wants badly to cross over to the world of Theseus, a world of 'theme' and 'thesis', a bright, clear, straightforward world compared to the dark and seemingly pointless meanderings of the labyrinth. The problem is that the bright, clear, straightforward world does not want her. Why? Would she make the straight lines crooked? Would she mix right and wrong? Would she be countertheme and antithesis?

Perhaps Dionysos comes to her because she has learned something from her adventure with Theseus. It may have been existentially necessary for her to make a bid for rationality and to discover for herself that the world of logical clarity, of ethical principle and spiritual achievement, can be as lacking in humanity as her dark world of feeling, instinct, and intuition. Does it mean that she is out of place in a man's world? Is he out of place in her world? Is there no way for her to function in the rational order without betraying her true nature? Is there no way for him to cope with irrational forces without pitting himself against them?

In what sense does Dionysos come for her and claim her for his own? It may be that the three versions of her story, that she died giving birth to Theseus' child, that she hung herself, that Dionysos found her abandoned and married her, are three aspects of a single outcome. According to Robert Graves, masks of Dionysos or little dolls representing the fertility Goddess were hung in vineyards and orchards in the belief that as the mask or doll turned in the wind, it would insure fertility wherever it looked.[12] Otto points out that only earth divinities are represented by masks, and that the meaning of the mask is confrontation, immediate presence, as opposed to the remoteness and inaccessibility of spiritual divinities.[13] There is something also to the fact that masks of Dionysos were not worn by human players, but were suspended from fruit trees. Could it be an archaic premonition of the mystery of the Crucifixion? A female attempt to join the green tree (the raw life-and-death which is Dionysos) and the hewn (bringing forth a son to the civilized man, Theseus)?

There is a fourth sister yet to be considered. Just as Agave and Autonoë are counterparts, represented on the horizontal arms of the cross, reaching out in the middle or human region, the dimension of breadth, so Semele and Ino are counterparts, represented on the vertical axis of the cross, as mother and foster-mother of Dionysos, who affirm the divine dimensions of height and depth. Through the power of Dionysos, Semele (simile) ascends into the heavenly heights, while in order to protect Dionysos, Ino (I know) plunges into the depths of the sea. There is an odd antithetical parallelism between Ino's plunge into the watery regions to protect the burgeoning female mind in the form of the horned serpent child from the destructive power of civilization, which here has its ultimate source in Hera's (self-)hatred, and the flight of the woman clothed with the sun, the moon beneath her feet, her head crowned with twelve stars, who takes refuge in the dry regions of the desert to protect the newborn male spirit from the depredations of the dragon-serpent (Rev. 12). The dry or spiritual woman is destined to remain hidden in the desert for twelve hundred and sixty days, that is, for three and one-half years or half the fullness of time. Is the wet or soulish woman destined to remain in the sea during that same period of time? Are we now approaching the other half of the fullness of time when male spirit and female soul will no longer be inimical to one another?

There are two versions of Ino's story. According to one version she married Athamas, the "reaper on high," and gave birth to two sons, Learchus and Melicertes. On a hunting expedition she was attacked by a lynx and in the process of killing it, she was seized by a Bacchic frenzy and wandered for a long while on Mt. Parnassus clad in nothing but its pelt. Finding her bloody clothes, her family thought her dead. Athamas meanwhile remarried a woman named Themisto, who also bore him twin sons. Later, Athamas learned that Ino was still alive and had her brought back to his home disguised as a nursemaid. Having learned the true identity of the nursemaid from her servants, Themisto plotted against her. She told the nursemaid to dress Ino's sons in mourning garments, but to dress her own sons in white wool. Meanwhile, Themisto told the guards to kill the twins dressed in mourning. Ino saw through the plot and switched the garments, so that it was Themisto's sons who were put to death. Athamas went mad when he learned of the murder. He shot Learchus with an arrow, mistaking him for a stag, while Ino escaped with Melicertes into the sea.

The lynx which triggers Ino's *mainomania* gets its name from eyes which shine in the dark. It is a fitting image for female mind, the light which shines in darkness (cf. Jn. 1:5). She is bound to Dionysos both passively through her long seizure and actively by her mothering of Melicertes to the point of sacrificing her own life. Even her loss of Learchus and her counterplot against the children of Themisto point to depths of motherhood. Her role as nursemaid in the story evokes memories of Demeter and Isis, who in their long search for the lost child (Persephone) and lost husband (Osiris) pose as nursemaids, playing a critical role as potential givers of immortality to the sons of the mother of the house. Does Ino confer immortality on Themisto's sons by consigning them to death? Is immortality the innermost meaning of the sacrifice of the firstborn? Is the nurse a greater mother (a *theotokos)* than the natural mother?

It is undoubtedly the bright eyes of the lynx which enable Ino to see through and defeat Themisto's plot, though not without loss on her own part. The play on which set of twins shall live and which shall die, or within a given set on which twin shall live and which shall die, makes me wonder if the story does not hark back to the Age of the Twins in the distant past. Its extreme archaic character seems further confirmed by the fact that irrational mind (Ino and her sons) wins out over the rational (Themisto ["theme" and "thesis"] and her sons). There is, however, a tragic premonition in the final turn of events. Because of the conflict, the truly mental part of irrational mind, Learchus, the "light principle," who as stag is the vehicle between earth and heaven, is lost and separated from the "sweet power" of irrational mind. It heralds a cleavage between the super-rational and sub-rational parts of irrational mind.

According to the other version of the story, Ino was Athamas' second wife. He first married Nephele, a cloud-form of Hera, who bore him a son, Phrixus, and a daughter, Helle. Nephele, whose name means "cloud" and appears to be kin to the Hebrew *nephesh* (soul), is a true anima figure, psychologically speaking, not only because she is a mirage of a Goddess, but also because she does not really love Athamas and seeks to use him to further her own purposes. By contrast, Ino is the flesh-and-blood wife who can both give and receive love. Resentful of the second marriage, Nephele demanded that the Boeotians sacrifice Athamas to Hera. While the Boeotian men procrastinated, Ino persuaded their wives to parch the seed-corn, causing the crops to fail. When Athamas sent messengers to Delphi to inquire after the reasons for the failure, Ino bribed the messengers to report that for a successful harvest Zeus required the sacrifice of Phrixus. The Boeotians were happy to put the finger on Phrixus because they believed the false report of Biadice, Phrixus' aunt, who had fallen in love with him and who, when rebuffed, had accused him of trying to rape her. Grieving, Athamas took Phrixus to a mountain top where he would have cut his throat had not a winged golden ram suddenly appeared to whisk Phrixus and Helle away. Helle fell from the ram's back into the straits between Europe and Asia, which were subsequently named for her, while the ram took Phrixus safely to Colchis, where it offered itself as sacrifice to Zeus and where Phrixus hung its golden fleece in the temple of Ares.

Then, deprived of her sacrifice, Hera afflicted Athamas with madness, causing him to mistake Learchus for the stag, shoot him with an arrow, and tear him limb from limb. Ino fled with her younger son, Melicertes, and Dionysos covered her escape by blinding Athamas, who flogged a she-goat in her stead. Meanwhile, Ino leaped with Melicertes into the sea and was deified.

It seems that the heavenly reaper loves all his children and wants to harmonize his two families, but is powerless to overcome the deadly enmity between his two wives, whether it be Ino versus Themisto (irrational versus rational) or Ino versus Nephele (irrational incarnate versus irrational spiritualized). The story of the conflict between Ino and Nephele appears to give the palm to Nephele, whose son, Phrixus, whose name means "bristling with horror" (at the Gorgon Face? at female religion?), survives through the ascendancy of the Ram. Phrixus seems to be a Greek version of Isaac and Joseph all rolled up in one. He represents the rise of moral consciousness with its horror of human sacrifice and its willingness to sacrifice the animal (instinctual life) in its place.[14] But what about Helle, who slides off the Ram's back and falls into the sea with Ino? Does the loss of the female along with the animal not count as human sacrifice? Do the frequent confusions of animal for human and human for animal suggest that with the loss of instinctual life something human is lost too?

The females of the story, whether goddess or mortal, are not discomfited by the prospect of human sacrifice. Their plots and counterplots have nothing to do with truth, justice, or moral principle of whatever kind. Their concern turns not upon whether but upon which of the males must die. Their allegiance is to something more elemental, bespeaking a consciousness which is genuinely religious, if amoral, of the mystery of life-and-death. It is a fundamental awareness that life requires death, that life is sustained by death, that if one lives, another must die. It is the wisdom behind the prophetic utterance of the fourth Gospel: "it is expedient for us, that one man should die for the people, and that the whole nation perish not" (Jn. 11:50). It makes it understandable that the males marked out for sacrifice (if not by one woman, then by another) should shrink away from female reality as from a religious horror. Is it not the spur which gives rise to patriarchal religion, marked as it is by the birth of moral consciousness and the hope of a separation of life from death?

If, however, we think of the struggle between male and female religion from the point of view of soul, there is a strange commonality in the mutual disregard. If the figure of woman's soul is male (animus), if the figure of man's soul is female (anima), then the two antithetical modes of religion are much alike in their despising of soul. In joy over the rescue of Phrixus there is little thought spared for the loss of Helle or of the golden ram. A mother under the spell of Dionysos destroys her own son, unable to distinguish human from animal, mind from instinct. Conversely, it may be that in a cultivation of soul lies hidden a secret of reconciliation between life-and-death and life over death. If so, a path of soul would also hold the key to a healing of the conflict between man and woman. But of first importance for woman, a path of soul, a conscious holding together of opposites, promises an answer to the deep-seated rift within woman, to the apparent enmity between what in her desires a full realization of her humanity and what belongs at all costs to the realm(s) of the superhuman and the subhuman.

Endnotes

1. Cf. F. E. Peters, *Greek Philosophical Terms: A Historical Lexicon* (New York: New York University Press 1967) under "noesis" and "nous."
2. Walter F. Otto, *Dionysus: Myth and Cult* (Dallas: Spring Publications, 1981), p. 61.
3. Hugh A. Moran, *The Alphabet and Ancient Signs* (Palo Alto, Cal.: Pacific Books, 1953), pp. 73–4.
4. The deep affinities between the mysteries of Christ and Dionysos were not lost on the earliest Greek converts to Christianity. Both are sons of a divine father and a human mother, the true vine, the wine changed to blood, the one who is dismembered (the breaking of the bread) in order to be remembered in the communion meal, etc.
5. 'Semele' is probably a form of a Thracian word *zemelo* meaning "earth", while 'Thyone', which has to do with ecstatic states (to rave, rage, etc.), comes from the root *dheu-*, which means "breath," hence soul or spirit, not only as a vital principle but as a principle of transcendence.
6. 'Dryas' is from the root *deru-*, which has as its concrete meaning "tree" and as its abstract meaning "true"; 'Learchus' is from the root *leuk-*, which is physical "light," but is also, as spiritual light, the *archon* or ruler of the mind.
7. Plato makes the point indirectly by having what was learned from Diotima follow upon 'Socrates' cross-examination of Agathon.
8. Cf. C. G. Jung. 1952. *Symbols of Transformation* in *Collected Works*, 5:459.
9. As derived from *medeon* or *medon*, her name means "ruler" or "queen"; as derived from *medea*, it means "cunning."
10. Cf. Joseph Campbell, *The Mythic Image* (Princeton: Princeton University Press, 1974), p. 118, and Heinrich Zimmer, *Myths and Symbols in Indian Art and Civilization* (Princeton: Princeton University Press, 1946), pp. 175–184.
11. See Jill Purce, *The Mystic Spiral* (New York: Thames and Hudson, 1974) and Theodore Schwenk, *Sensitive Chaos* (New York: Schocken Books, 1965).
12. Robert Graves, *Greek Myths* (Baltimore: Penguin, 1955), 98.5, 79.2, 88.10.
13. Otto, ch. 6, pp. 86–91.
14. According to Robert Graves (*Greek Myths* 70.5), Melicertes = Melkarth = Moloch (cf. Leviticus 18:21; I Kings 11:7; II Kings 23:13). In Carthage the term *molk* designated infant sacrifice.

Chapter Four

Untitled

The scene changes. In a darkened movie theater a small boy dressed in knickers, knee socks, and a touring cap is scrambling around beneath the seats, looking for a bit of film. The curl of film which he has not yet found is about twelve to fifteen inches long.

At first I was uncertain whether this scene belonged to the dream of the woman with the hole in her chest or made up a separate dream on its own. After some reflection I decided that it did not matter which way I took it. Since it follows hard upon the initial dream it needs to be considered in connection with the dream of the woman, one way or another. I noticed that the dream of the woman falls quite naturally into three parts: the initial image, the question "Is this it?" and the response "No, that is not it." The scene involving the young boy relates to that triad as what Jung would call "the recalcitrant fourth."

Jung notes that in western culture there is a characteristic "wavering" between three and four. I also wavered momentarily because I could not see the connection between the two scenes. Yet from the beginning there has been a felt conviction not only that they belong together, but that the second scene holds the secret solution to the enigma posed by the first. The fact that I opted to include the fourth element as essential to the first three places me firmly within a feminine mode of mind, since three is traditionally a male number while four is female. I notice, however, an inversion: my three focuses on the woman with the hole in her chest, while my fourth focuses on the effort of the young boy.[1] It is doubtless a typical instance of female psychology at work, where the three stand forth in the light of day (consciously female) while the fourth gropes in the dark (unconsciously male).

I marvel that despite my long schooling in Christianity with its option for a male Trinity and its discomfiture with the fourth, which

73

must be either the devil or woman, or both (Eve and her snake), my unconscious dream life moves inexorably along a path of its own choosing. Where would I be if I ignored the recalcitrant fourth? Jung notes that where the fourth is missing, as in the case of Plato revealed in the opening line of the *Timaeus* ("One, two, three—but where, my dear Timaeus, is the fourth of those guests of yesterday who were to entertain me today?"),[2] things remain up in the air, intellectualized, a word not yet made flesh, for it is a function of the fourth to confer materiality. Already I notice that my style has changed as I begin the fourth chapter, becoming more personal.

It has always puzzled me how Christianity, which insists that the incarnation of God is at the center of its mystery, is nevertheless so ill at ease with the flesh, which it identifies with woman and with sin. Now I turn that puzzle on its head and wonder how I or any woman can find her way in such a hostile environment. I look at the Holy Mother of God, the Theotokos, who surrounds the Godhead like a nimbus, and realize that there is no way to God or to one's own self except through the troublesome fourth. However man may learn to cope with female flesh, she finds her way through by containing the hostile male spirit. "for the LORD hath created a new thing in the earth, A woman shall compass a man" (Jer. 31:22).[3] Now in the empty hole is placed an irritant like a grain of sand in an oyster. If I can only manage to contain the writhing monster without letting go or pushing it away from me, like Athena, in disgust, a slow transformation process will surely occur. If I can keep all those hateful words in my heart and ponder them, what response will they generate?

The boy is contained in the dark and empty THEAter. Is it an accident that the place where a showing which compels the gaze occurs is also the body of the Goddess? More specifically, it is a movie theater. Not a place where "live" theater occurs, the reflected action and reaction of daytime life which make up the drama of consciousness, but a place where images are projected on a large screen corresponding to the nighttime drama of dreams. The art of film and Freud's *Interpretation of Dreams* emerged hand-in-hand as twin heralds of the twentieth century. While cinema is a product of art and the dream is a product of nature, making it both less and more than art, I wonder if our dream life is not the secret school at which the art of film is learned (art as an imitation of nature) by its innovators and from which it derives its magic. Whether films in their turn have a reciprocal influence on dream life is another question. Sometimes I think that a desire to go to the movies arises from a need to nourish or to supplement one's dream life. For me at least, a good movie has a spellbinding quality and a capacity for transport equalled only by a powerful novel. Aside from the most interesting correlation between the average length of a movie (90 minutes) and the duration of REM periods of sleep, there is in both the film and the dream a magnification of the image, a freedom of movement in space and time and an easy blend of fantasy and reality.

In particular the fluidity of the camera, its ability to move from long to medium to extremely close range, to race and to freeze, to sharpen or dissolve, to shift points of view, and the kind of natural identification which takes place between the viewer and the camera ("I am a Camera"), bear an uncanny resemblance to the dream process where sometimes I am a character in my dream, sometimes I shift identities from one character to another, and sometimes I am an invisible spectator. Who is dreaming the dream and who is being dreamed? In my own dream I both am and am not the woman with the hole in her chest. Am I and am I not also her lover? Am I and am I not the voice which she addresses and which addresses her? I both am and am not the empty dark theater where the young boy searches. Am I and am I not also the boy? And the image for which he searches? Am I and am I not the dreamer? And am I and am I not the interpreter of the dream?

Perhaps it would be best to think of dream consciousness after the manner of the *Upanishads:* as an intermediate state between ordinary waking consciousness with its identification with ego and the deeper awareness of Self. It would make the blurring of boundaries between subject and object and between the personal and the collective which occurs while dreaming more understandable. And what is it that functions as "go-between" ego and Self if not the soul? The soul as dreamer and dream is contrasexual (the anima as spinner and web, the animus as magician and light show), is the recalcitrant fourth, and, according to Jung, operates in the mode of the so-called "inferior function," the function—whether it be thinking or feeling (rational functions), sensation or intuition (irrational functions)—which remains least accessible to consciousness, awkward and uncontrollable. I notice that the boy in my dream is crawling on the floor beneath the seats either on his hands and knees or maybe even on his belly, like the snake. It seems to indicate that the function in me which is missing or hard to find, impossible to manage, is sensation. I realize that I may be hasty in blaming Christianity for the loss of something which is a naturally missing element in my own personality and which it has merely (or not so merely) reinforced. Does religion then militate against the soul? What an irony that would be since religion purports to save the soul.

Or perhaps it is more in the nature of a paradox that, like some medicines, religion is both poison and cure. Whichever function is in question it works both for and against. It is the bearer of the highest values and the harshest judgments, the most sublime inspirations and the most superstitious beliefs; it is a spur to thought and forbids thought. It both exalts and execrates the flesh. Or perhaps it is not so strange that religion should claim to "save the soul," since it is altogether like anima and animus, ambivalent, working both for and against, uniting high and low in the "between" mode, dangerous but indispensable.[4]

By situating the place in a movie theater and having the boy search for a bit of film, I think the dream is turning my attention from content to form, which means, from a philosophic point of view, that the recalcitrant fourth, if I may take this instance as paradigmatic, functions on a "meta" level. It induces that reflexive look from object back towards subject which we associate with self-awareness.[5] It would mean that the function least amenable to consciousness is that through which consciousness in the full psychological sense of the Delphic oracle ("Know thyself") is reached. It would mean that the function which hinders our progress is that whereby we transcend.

If the fourth confers materiality, it seems to me that in my case at least, and I think it would be so for all women, the contrasexual element is the dynamic factor as well. It may be universally true for men as well as for women, if we consider how Shakti is the *dynamis* for Shiva in kundalini yoga. The serpent power, male for women, female for men, is that which shoots up and down, uniting heights and depths. The boy in my dream is on the move, groping, feeling his way in the darkness, or as the dream chooses to put it, is "scrambling around beneath the seats." The various meanings of 'scramble' are suggestive of the kundalini energy in certain respects. A scramble is a climb upward, an urgent or ardent struggle. An interesting military use of the word means to take off with all possible haste to intercept enemy aircraft. But it also has negative connotations of mixing up or throwing together confusedly, scattering as well as collecting, gathering in a hurried or disorderly fashion, and in electronics of distorting or garbling a signal so that it is rendered unintelligible without a special receiver or knowledge of a code. It is a kind of free-for-all struggle where it is very uncertain which element will predominate, or what will be saved and what lost or trampled in the melee.

The word 'scramble' is itself an amalgam, a blend of two obsolete words 'scamble', which means to struggle for, and 'cramble', to crawl.

Here are the two principal elements: a struggle upward, pointing to the kundalini energy itself, its direction and its ardor, and the mode of that struggle, a crawl on hands and knees. It is in my case a mode of discovery which has little to do with seeing and hearing, but much to do with touch, full body contact with an emphasis on the hands. It is the hands and fingers which must find and identify the bit of film, although the hands will not be able to "see" what they have found. It is a peculiarity of cinema that the image must be projected on a screen by means of a light before it can be seen. It is also a peculiarity of imagination that it is a projecting faculty. It translates amorphous "in here" feelings into "out there" forms to that we can see them and relate to them consciously. Cinema is like an imperfect mechanical imitation of imagination, the dreaming faculty, somewhat the way our mechanical earthmovers and sky travelers are imitators of insect forms.

But I don't want to leave the word 'scramble' just yet or the clues it may give me to the kundalini force and the work of the animus. The crawling and confusion connoted by 'scramble' remind me of Psyche's first task, the work of the ants sorting the grains. It was too subtle a work to be accomplished at the gross level of ordinary consciousness. It required a finesse and an ability to work on many fronts at once which the ants by their tiny size and multiplicity could do. Psyche had to entrust herself to the process, providing as it were the container in which it might occur. The awakening of the kundalini (and notice that the boy is moving "beneath the seats" at the root chakra) is thought to be a subtle reconditioning of the nervous system, a work which may be both painful and frightening.[6] I may feel like I am being scrambled; "my brains are scrambled." There may be an experience of confusion and disorder. Things may start moving too fast. What held together previously may now fly apart; what did not belong together may now wake up bedfellows. A world comes apart and reassembles itself. "He" thrashes about threatening everything and "She" provides a safe place where the work may occur and concentrate.

The boy's dress is made distinctive by the knickers, knee socks, and touring cap. It makes me think of child movie stars in the early days of film, like Jackie Coogan and Mickey Rooney. It also reminds me of photographs of my own father as a young boy. The boy is on the one hand the personification of the dream as cinema, as the pro-jected and magnified image of nighttime consciousness. On the other hand he is both the father of the woman and, according to dream logic, the son of the woman and her lover. A boy who is both father and son would have to be a divine child,[7] but Psyche's child has a questionable status because of her infidelity. "And a little child shall lead them" (Is. 11:6); can one follow the guidance of such a child in safety? It raises the question of the truth of dreams, and for me in particular it raises the question of the truth of my own dream, whether I should look to my dream, existentially and religiously, for guidance.

From the ancient world we have inherited a certain double-mindedness about dreams. In Greek popular religion dreams were taken seriously; dream incubation was practised—somewhat akin to the American Indian tradition of searching for a vision—as a method of healing in the temples of Asklepios. Among the elite a more rational turn of mind prevailed, as witnessed by both Homer (Od. XIX, 562) and Virgil (Aen. VI, 894 sq.) who spoke of two gates through which dreams may pass. True dreams come through the gate of horn while false dreams come through the gate of ivory. Ivory being more precious than horn (though horn is an extremely ancient symbol of supernatural power and radiance), the dreams which come through the gate of ivory are those which are "too good to be true," which is what Penelope says of her dream of the geese. Actually, the happy ending which the dream promises and of which she despairs does come true, for the stranger to whom she recounts the dream is the long lost Odysseus himself. But if Homer doubted the truth of dreams, the doubt had metastasized to full-blown despair by the time of Virgil. In the Bible also we find a profound ambivalence with regard to the productions of the irrational mind. The use of irrational methods to know the mind of God, practices such as divination, soothsaying, and ordeals, are roundly condemned, and yet the path charted by the Bible in both Old and New Testaments is marked by prophetic dreams as by so many milestones, while revelation itself is a manifestly irrational phenomenon.

It seems that in Old Testament times the interests of a monotheism interpreted as an exclusive One rather than an inclusive One militated against the free flow of spirit predicted by the prophet Joel (2:28–29), while in New Testament times the Pentecostal outbreak of spirit was by the second century curbed in favor of a juridical localization of the Holy Spirit in the person of Church authorities. When that same spirit burst its bonds at the time of the Protestant Reformation, it was once again hastily corralled in the form of a definitive book, the Bible, to which nothing could be added, nothing taken away. The rational mind loves boundaries and fears, with good reason, the boundless influx of the unconscious. Who knows where it might take us? And to what end, salvation or destruction?

Religious directors of conscience have worked out certain guide-lines for dealing with these irruptions from beyond the bounds.[8] Ob-jectively, a personal revelation must be consistent with the received tradition; subjectively, it should lead not to disturbance of soul and vanity, but to greater peace of soul and to a higher level of integrity. These are excellent guidelines from a psychological point of view. The first avoids the danger of dissociation, a splitting of the personality and a rending from one's social context and ancestral ground. The second avoids the danger of psychic inflation, of identifying with or calling "mine" what comes from beyond the bounds and forgetting about the inevitable boundaries or limitations which serve to bring one back down to earth and to the daily miseries. All of this is well and good so long as the insistence on consistency does not stifle the spirit and the in-sistence on humility does not break the spirit. We might ask ourselves to what extent was Jesus rejected by his contemporaries because both in his person and his teaching he appeared to be at odds with his tradition? "You have been told . . . but I say to you." What was the nature of the inconsistency? Did it betray the essence of the tradition or carry it forward according to its ownmost truth?

I believe my principle of containment to be a way, a female way, of avoiding the dangers of dissociation and inflation while at the same time both allowing and encouraging a stirring of the spirit. It would be achieved by containing as much as possible of what has gone before. Not just the dominant elements of what has gone before, which in my case would be Christianity, the Roman Catholic version in particular, and the culture of the European West, but also the minority voices of the present and the half-forgotten voices of the past out of which the future springs and which are asking to be heard—woman's voice, the voice of the American Indian, of the black, voices from the southern hemisphere, from the far east, animal voices, elemental voices, primal voices, what Jung calls "the voices of the Unanswered, Unresolved, and Unredeemed."[9] Holding them all together, what I love and what I hate, what loves me and what hates me; containing that all,[10] it con-centrates and begins to move. Blessing the container which concen-trates, I do not forget that it also limits.

The second danger, that of inflation or vanity, to call it by its old name, takes me back to the distinction between horn and ivory. One major difference between the two is that ivory has a high cash value; one can "cash in" on it. In that case the true purpose of the dream may be subverted to further the ambitions of the ego. Integrity, on the other hand, implies that everything and everyone start coming together without predominance of any one. It is a curious state of mind and heart where judgment of truth and value seem to diminish, but where attention and openness are magnified, where detachment and enjoyment go hand in hand. What is happening is a balancing of rational and irrational functions or, to put it in more current language, a synthesizing of the two sides of the brain.[11] Once the frightening strangeness of the change has passed, a great and in some ways unshakeable peace of soul ensues. I say "in some ways" unshakeable because the process of integration must be repeated as each new challenge to the boundaries of the container appears.

What must be avoided is not only a rigid consistency which stifles the spirit, a past without a future, but peace of soul too cheaply bought. Any time the boundaries are challenged there is an initial, perhaps even a prolonged disturbance. But how could a higher level of integration come to pass without a preliminary disruption of the lower order? Two points to bear in mind, both etymological: soul is "breath" and soul is "life." There must be room to breathe and agitation to stir up life. A startle, a gasp, a discovery.

What is the integrating factor? To what magnetic center are the previously disparate elements drawn and what is it which seeks to balance what is out of balance? Or, to put it more existentially, what do we experience when we go through breakdown and re-creation? In the process we are at the mercy of something too powerful to resist and which we cannot understand. It may be called God, it may be called the Self; it may be called by other names or no name. It takes us from one egoic point of view to another egoic point of view. In the process, while we are drowning and undergoing a sea change, we approximate Reality itself. Once the storm calms and we are cast safely ashore, we achieve a new consciousness, a new self-possession, which is nonetheless just a point of view, deepened and expanded (an enlarged container), but still infinitely short of what it seeks to envision. In the lostness I, along with everything else, swirl dizzily around God; in the foundness there is a partial coming together of things, 'God' included ("my God"), around me. There is a most real sense in which losing is greater than finding. It opens up the meaning of certain mystical utterances, such as Lao Tzu's "one gains by losing/ and loses by gaining" (#42) and Jesus' "whosoever shall seek to save his life shall lose it; and whosoever shall lose his life shall preserve it" (Lk. 17:33).

If Jung is right in thinking that at least one of the principal functions of the dream is to compensate the one-sidedness of ordinary consciousness, it may be seen as an important if not indispensable contributor towards the pursuit of truth and salvation. "The unconscious is the unknown at any given moment, so it is not surprising that dreams add to the conscious psychological situation of the moment all those aspects which are essential for a totally different point of view" (8: 469). Dreams are not the only compensators, of course. Our personal and political conflicts with "others" in outer life exhibit the one-sidedness of our point of view all too well. But the dream is a gift in an unusual wrapping. It is a small gift, secret, personal, not too intrusive but with strings attached. The other side of a gift is a task. Do we need dreams? What is their special contribution? Dreams are the unconscious corollaries of thoughts while conflicts are the unconscious corollaries of actions. Action requires thought to be human action, so perhaps conflict requires the dream to be a fully human drama. There is a story in the making, "just a story" as Plato would say, and we all know that "telling a story" is telling a lie, but these fictions are closer to the truth than our facts and the soul thrives on a good story.

Working with the dream is a way of keeping the process going of breakdown and re-creation, of coming and going between the greater and lesser reality, much like the exhalation and inhalation of breath, which is soul. Working with my own dream I find first of all one great enigmatic image, that of a woman with a hole in her chest. I sense that it is a great image, telling me something not only about myself but about other women as well, and about whatever reality is associated with "woman." I begin to explore the image, following certain pathways of association which occur to me, realizing that there are any number of possible pathways which I am leaving unexplored. The image expands into a story, the tightly compressed story of the dream. As I stare at the images and reflect on the happenings of my dream story, the images connect to other stories still circulating in the long memory of humankind. Back and forth I go between the dream story and the older stories, the one casting light into the shadows of the other. Questions surface and feelings, connections are made weaving me into the great web of story, thoughts slowly form like blessed solutions to the suffering and uncertainty of my life. Here I sit now with the still loose threads in my hands, ready to tie off the knots of my weaving. And a way to make those knots has been given to me. It has to do with the problem of the three and the four, symbolically resolved by a woman with the marvelous name of Maria Prophetissa, the Jewess or Copt. Maria's formula, often quoted by Jung and pondered by alchemists for over a thousand years, is: "One becomes two, two becomes three, and out of the Third comes the One as the Fourth."

"One becomes two": One is the image of the woman with the hole in her chest. Or perhaps I should say "zero," since 0 is the female complement to the phallic 1 and expresses the hole. Two is the woman and her lover, who is the serpent-Dionysos-Christ-Eros. And now I come to the first loose thread, realizing that I have yet to make more than a hint at connections between these many versions of the animus. That there is a connection in the human imagination (and not just in my own subjectivity) is well established from the literature. Biblical imagery, echoed in Christian art, establishes the connection between the serpent and Christ; Greek mythology crowns Dionysos with serpents and Eros is prophesied to be a viper. There is an amazing overlap of imagery between the attributes of Christ and Dionysos, all the more amazing since Dionysos is a chthonic deity and Christ is spirit. The wounded, open, life-giving source which is the Heart of Christ is surely Eros, the son of Poverty and Plenty (according to Plato). What about Dionysos and Eros? I have yet to do more than drop a dark hint, which I scarcely understand, that Eros is Dionysos made conscious.

I notice that the animus figures run the gamut from beast (the serpent, Beast) to man-beast (Actaeon and Pentheus, the Minotaur) to God-beast (Dionysos) to God-man (Christ) to an interiorized principle of life and love (Eros). By all the multiple allusions back and forth I discover that the animus stretches unbroken from beast through man and God to principle. I begin to realize that the one does not cancel out the other. It is possible to be both beastly and humane, to be godly and to be "human all-too-human," to be both an outer reality (an "other") and an inner reality (the principle of "my" life and "my" love). My lust, my love, and my Love. In Plato's *Symposium* the argument turns explicitly on whether Eros is divine or human and implicitly on whether Eros is the same as oneself or other; the Cretan drama turns on whether man or beast shall prevail at the center of the labyrinth and in its outer reaches; the Theban drama turns on whether the outcome will be divine or merely human, beastly or humane. All of these issues are taken up again and spiritualized (breathed anew) in the Christian drama. The answer is never a straightforward choice between one possibility and another; it always seems to be a paradoxical "yes" to all the options.

It is difficult to hold on to such a thought. The logical mind always wants to sunder what imagination has joined together: "if this, then not that." But the contemplative mind which stares wide-eyed or with half-closed eyes at the images is held by the storied thought. Rather than holding (as in a vise or with pincers, in one's fist, pocket, or purse, so that it does not move or change shape, get lost or out of control), one beholds. "Behold the Lamb of God [God-Beast], which taketh away the sin [the sundering] of the world" (Jn. 1:29). The prefix 'be-' in 'behold' indicates "thoroughness," as though one can behold more thoroughly than one can hold; "on all sides," as though in defiance of the uncertainty principle which maintains that if a fix is made on one feature of reality, another feature is lost sight of; "in relation to" and "away from," connected and disconnected, the same and the other.

The early centuries of the Christian era were characterized by the wide-eyed, Byzantine stare. It is consciousness mesmerized or held by the image. By contrast, the modern or post-Christian era has been characterized by the closed eye if not by the covered eye, like the monkey who sees no evil. It is the shadow side of an over-emphasis on the rational mind, stretching from Kant's distinction between the reality (noumenon) and the image (phenomenon) to Hegel's reduction of the reality to the image through self-appropriation, which psychology calls "withdrawal of the projection." Perhaps the present moment (post-modern and post–post-Christian) may be characterized by the half-closed eye, which we see in images of the Buddha. Half-closed eyes look both inward and outward, beholding rather than holding or being held, recognizing that "yes, it is this," "yes, it is that;" "no, it is not this," "no, it is not that."

The reality of Dionysos spans from beast to man to God but with more emphasis on beast and God, oscillating horrifically between the two, and less on man. It is true that Dionysos is the son of a woman, more often than not represented in human shape and with great dignity, like the calm eye in the midst of a storm of maenads, satyrs, and sileni. Even so, the impact of Dionysos on human beings is a joining of extremes (God-Beast) in unconsciousness, that is, in a momentary loss of humanity. The reality of Christ also spans from beast (Lamb of God, the serpent lifted up) to man to God but with more emphasis on man and God, the spiritual man, and less on beast. The beastly side is revealed in the Sacrifice of the Cross and the shared Communion meal, but the Christian rite is performed symbolically, not in the bloodiness of a maenadic orgy. Dionysos' lack of humanity and Christ's lack of animality[12] point to a remaining blind spot in western consciousness, which I believe relates on the underside to our continuing difficulty in distinguishing and reconciling outer and inner realities.

But that difficulty spurs on the process. "Two becomes three": what is left out becomes angry and bangs at the door for recognition. "Behold, I stand at the door, and knock" (Rev. 3:20). What is left out shows up in the women in devilish anger (woman as *locus* of the devil; female consciousness as manifestation of male unconsciousness, and vice-versa). The anger of Semele's sisters is expressed overtly as religious indignation that what is merely human should call itself divine, but covertly (in the sons) reveals itself to be anger over what of the human (rationality, moderation, self-control) has been left out. The anger of Hera and Aphrodite is expressed overtly as outrage over a usurpation of their divine prerogatives (the divine consort and divine beauty), but covertly reveals itself to be anger over what of their human domain (mistress of domestic values and mistress of the civilized arts) has been left out of consideration. Psyche's sisters and Beauty's sisters were at first thankful to have been spared a beastly fate, to be able to enjoy a normal human life with normal husbands, but were chagrined to discover that what appeared beastly was in fact divine. What they resent is the lack of human justice. How is it fair that Psyche and Beauty, who were more richly endowed by nature, should also enjoy a happier fate? Is it fair that the rich get richer and the poor get poorer? They are determined to interject human justice somehow, to force Psyche and Beauty to earn their happiness and to become fully human in the process. They are really furious that Beast is not beastly enough and know in some dark way that true humanity cannot be reached except through enduring the beastly burden of the flesh. In the earlier story there is more darkness than light (the tragic *dénouement*), in the later stories there is more light than darkness (the happy ending), but in both earlier and later stories there is a kind of fullness, a running realization, if half-conscious, that what is hardly thinkable, a conjoining of rational and irrational, is nonetheless necessary for the fulfillment of heart's desire (Eros). Without the one *and* the other, there would be no story, and soul requires a good story.

Now comes the difficult part. "Out of the Third comes the One as the Fourth." The first thing I notice is that oneness comes out of the wicked Third. In the Christian Trinity the Third is the Holy Spirit, but the psychological character of the Third indicates that the Spirit is not holy in the way we think, but is rather the bringer of wholeness. Psychologically, we are more prone to identify the Third with the devil. The implication is that there is a secret connection between the disruptive principle (the devil) and the unifying principle (the Holy Spirit). The Holy Spirit is often described as what is between the Father and the Son. It should be read as what "comes between" the Father and the Son, the problematic in their relationship, and only then as the love which binds them. Not only does life arise out of conflict, according to the wisdom of Heraclitus, but love as well.

Corresponding to the divine Trinity of Father, Son, and Holy Spirit, but even better to the psychological trinity of Father and two sons, Christ and the Devil,[13] is my female trinity which would doubtless form a downward pointing triangle reflecting the female pubic region.The mysterious woman with the hole in her chest would be at the bottommost point of the triangle, her central emptiness (0) corresponding to the divine pleroma (1). Her nought and the Father's fullness are not the One of which Maria's formula speaks because still unconscious, out of the human range. She then unfolds into good earth (Semele-Psyche-Beauty), corresponding to the woman's healing, and bad earth (the outraged Goddesses and the enraged sisters), corresponding to what in the woman remains unredeemed but seeks redemption. Good earth is the female equivalent of Christ and bad earth is the female equivalent of the Devil.

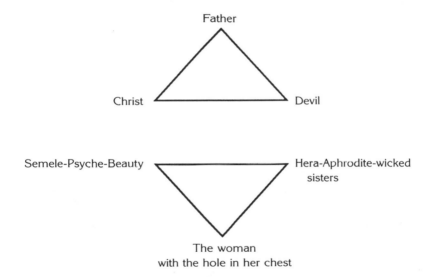

It is the arrival of the male figure which provokes or makes explicit the split between the good and wicked sisters, just as it is only when the eternal Son becomes a man in time through MATERialization that the devil can appear to tempt him (from 2 to 3 by way of 4). If the fourth is embraced, the double triangle becomes a single square.

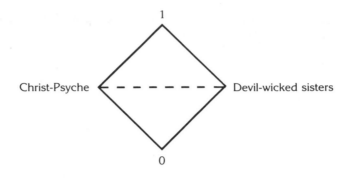

If the necessity of the third is recognized or made conscious, if it is realized that human oneness comes out of the third, and not without it, as the fourth, then that oneness is achieved in the kundalini lightning-flash. Notice that the divine polarities (0 and 1) are only joined by means of a human reconciliation of good and evil in the zigzag of the lightning-flash.[14] It is not to say that there is no implicit vertical pole joining 0 and 1 eternally, but conscious oneness requires human cooperation. Female enlightenment flashes from zero to one (the Pleroma), while male enlightenment flashes from one to zero (the Kenosis). Human enlightenment joins male to female: zero is one and one is zero; in the Kenosis there is Pleroma and in the Pleroma is Kenosis.

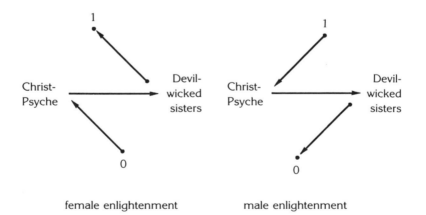

female enlightenment   male enlightenment

The child born of this union is both human and divine. Just as important, he is the child not only of Psyche and Christ but of the Devil and the wicked sisters. In the stories revolving around Ino the union was not complete. There were always two sons, twins, so very close to oneness but moving apart, experiencing opposite fates. A choice had to be made between male and female when Helle fell into the sea but Phrixus was saved, between the sons of which mother as in the conflict between Ino and Nephele and between Ino and Themisto, and between the sons of a single mother when Learchus was lost but Melicertes saved. But, to paraphrase Lao Tzu and Anaximander, what moves far apart must return. Male and female, divine and human, rational and irrational, truth and sweet power must come back together. Later stories will begin to sound the theme.

What is the bit of film which the boy seeks? There is no way of knowing until he finds it, whence the title of this chapter, "Untitled." I know however that it is there to be found because "I" saw it, a curl of film about twelve to fifteen inches long, beneath the seats. A filmmaker friend of mine told me that a piece of film that long would probably contain only one image. The most I can know at this point is that the image is there as a genuine possibility to be realized existentially and that the image is one.

It may be that the unknownness of the unifying image just reflects where I am and am not in my own journey, my own difficulty with the recalcitrant fourth, but it may have other meanings as well which reflect us all and the times in which we live. I have often thought about why in contemporary art so many pieces are entitled "Untitled." I can think of a number of reasons, all of which have something to say about our times as a moment of shift to another level of consciousness: (1) the artist is working out of the unconscious and so does not know fully what he or she is doing as opposed to realizing a preconceived idea; (2) the artist wishes to give the viewer/auditor maximum freedom of interpretation ("what" is experienced depends upon "who" is experiencing and is a revelation of that "who"); (3) a title would limit and prestructure the experience and/or interpretation unnecessarily (a sense of "more" to be discovered); (4) the artist wishes to put the accent on experience, to encourage the viewer/auditor to stay with the experience, whereas a title causes one to leap from experience to (outworn) interpretation; (5) staying with an unnamed experience leads to subtler levels of experience and to transformative shifts at those subtle levels; (6) . . . ?

The dream is unfinished. Lessing once said that if God held forth to him all truth in his right hand and in his left the lifelong pursuit of it, he would choose the left hand. My female self quite naturally prefers the left hand of God, the unfinishedness which allows for further discovery and further growth, for the emergence of the "who" and its unboundedness. She has a feel more for the unsaid than for the said. But my male soul wants and seeks the right hand as well. Without his determination there would be no spur and direction to growth, even if that direction is unseen but must be groped after on hands and knees. For now it is enough to know that the image is there somewhere to be found, and that the seeking is not in vain.

Endnotes

1. For a female trinity and a male fourth see Jung in *Collected Works* 14: 563 and 16:533. See also ch. 1, sec. 5, for the female trinity of water, blood, and Spirit.
2. Cornford's translation.
3. See also the 15th c. *Vierge ouvrante* from the Musée de Cluny, which appears in so many of Joseph Campbell's works (e.g., in *The Mythic Image*, pp. 60–61). It is a carved wood statue of the Virgin holding the Infant Christ in her right arm and the world in her left hand. The statue opens down the middle to reveal the divine Trinity within.
4. The word 'religion' from Latin *religio,* a bond between human and God, comes from *re-*, back, + *ligare,* to bind or fasten.
5. Cf. the brain folding back upon itself, reflexive verbs and pronouns, the dream as mirror.
6. Cf. Gopi Krishna, *Kundalini: The Evolutionary Energy in Man* (Boston: Shambala, 1971) and Lee Sannella, *Kundalini—Psychosis or Transcendence?* (San Francisco: H. S. Dakin, 1976).
7. Incestuous relationships are a symbolic hallmark of divinity. Cf. Dante's reference to Mary as "Virgin Mother, daughter of thine own son. . . ." (*Paradiso*, 31. 1–2.) *The Divine Comedy,* Norton trans. III, 252, cited in Joseph Campbell, *The Mythic Image,* p. 197.
8. Cf. Jung in *Collected Works* 11:32n.
9. C. G. Jung, *Memories, Dreams, Reflections* (New York: Pantheon Books, 1961), p. 191.
10. Naturally the "all" is an ideal which can only be approached, not achieved. But it can function in practice as a guiding principle or norm. The reader will see that what I am working towards, religiously, is an inclusive One rather than an exclusive One.
11. The balancing could occur the other way around, a diminishing of irrational functions in favor of rational if what is needed is more ability to discriminate between true and false, good and evil. In general, what the West seeks at this moment of its history is an enhancement of the irrational functions, right brain development, to counterbalance an overdevelopment of and reliance upon the rational left brain.
12. For a bold and insightful reminder see Leo Steinberg's *Sexuality of Christ in Renaissance Art and in Modern Oblivion* (New York: Pantheon Books, 1983).
13. Cf. Jung in *Collected Works* 11:256.
14. The lightning-flash is a reappearance of the snake.

Index